Poetry: Powerful Thoughts in Tiny Packages

DEDICATION

To Kate Montgomery, who imagined and inspired and led the creation of this series.

FirstHand
An imprint of Heinemann
A division of Reed Elsevier Inc.
361 Hanover Street
Portsmouth, NH 03801-3912
www.heinemann.com

Offices and agents throughout the world

Photography: Peter Cunningham

The author and publisher wish to thank those who have generously given permission to reprint borrowed material:

"Safety Pin," "Aquarium" and "cow" from *All the Small Poems and Fourteen More* by Valerie Worth. Copyright © 1987, 1994 by Valerie Worth. Reprinted by permission of Farrar, Straus and Giroux, LLC.

"Way Down in the Music," "Things," and "Rope Rhyme" from *Honey, I Love* by Eloise Greenfield. Text Copyright © 1978 by Eloise Greenfield. Used by permission of HarperCollins Publishers.

Continued on page 134.

Library of Congress Cataloging-in-Publication Data

Calkins, Lucy McCormick.
   Poetry : powerful thoughts in tiny packages / Lucy Calkins and Stephanie Parsons.
   p. cm. — (Units of study for primary writing ; 7)
   ISBN 0-325-00531-1 (pbk. : alk. paper)
   1. English language-Composition and exercises-Study and teaching (Primary)—United States. 2. Poetry-Authorship-Study and teaching (Primary)—United States. 3. Curriculum planning-United States. I. Parsons, Stephanie. II. Title.
   LB1529.U5C356 2003   2003019536
   372.62'3--dc22

Printed in the United States of America on acid-free paper

07   06   05   ML   4   5

SERIES COMPONENTS

▶ **The Nuts and Bolts of Teaching Writing** provides a comprehensive overview of the processes and structures of the primary writing workshop.

▶ You'll use **The Conferring Handbook** as you work with individual students to identify and address specific writing issues.

▶ The seven **Units of Study**, each covering approximately four weeks of instruction, give you the strategies, lesson plans, and tools you'll need to teach writing to your students in powerful, lasting ways. Presented sequentially, the Units take your children from oral and pictorial story telling, through emergent and into fluent writing.

▶ To support your writing program, the **Resources for Primary Writers CD-ROM** provides video and print resources. You'll find clips of the authors teaching some of the lessons, booklists, supplementary material, **reproducibles** and **overheads**.

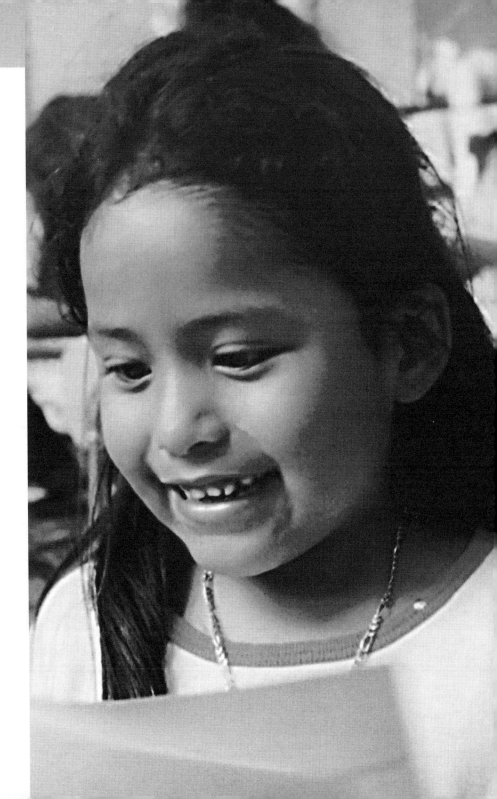

POETRY: POWERFUL THOUGHTS IN TINY PACKAGES

On summer evenings when I was little, I used to get on my bike and spin around the neighborhood calling, "Games in the circle at 7:00, games in the circle at 7:00." Then as day turned to dusk, whoever was "it" would close his or her eyes, one of us would kick the can, and we'd all race to hide in hedges and bushes. Some of us would be found, and we would convene in the circular driveway. Then, in the final moment, there would be the call, "Come out, come out wherever you are," and the others would emerge—one dropping from a low hanging tree branch, another rising up from the back seat of a car. Soon we'd all gather in the driveway.

When we teach young children to write poetry, it is as if someone has called, "Come out, come out, wherever you are." Children do emerge, each from his or her separate hiding spot, and as a class, we convene as a community of poets.

In classrooms across the world, very young children write poems that astonish us. "How is it possible?" we ask. How can young, untutored minds write poems like this one, written by a five-year-old from a Bronx kindergarten?

> I am the kind of writer who writes
>   in peace and quiet.
> I am the kind of writer who really feels
>   the rain and the wind.
> That feeling makes me want to sway from
>   one way to another.
> It's all in the heart.

Perhaps part of the answer is that poetry is the genre of childhood. When I was very little, it fell to my Dad to give my sisters and me our baths. He'd line three of us up in the tub, and then bring us out, one at a time, for the drying ritual. With one hand on each end of the towel, he'd rub us down as if he was the shoe-shine man, pulling his towel this way and that way. Meanwhile, we'd spin and dance in delight. "Skiddley dinky, dinky do—I love you," he'd croon. "I love you in the morning and in the afternoon. I love you in the sunshine and in the rainstorms too. Skiddley dinky, dinky do—I love you."

There were poems about table manners—"Lucy, Lucy, strong and able, keep your elbows off the table." There were poems to accompany our evening games in the circle, "Red Rover, Red Rover, send Barry right over. . . ." When we went to weddings (those beloved events where we all felt like brides), we'd watch big-eyed as the grown ups recited poems to each other. "I, Sally, take you, Tom, to be my wedded husband. . . ."

Why This Unit?

When designing a unit of study on poetry, the first and most fundamental question may be, "What can this particular unit give to our children? What new work will children do within this unit of study?"

For Stephanie Parsons, first grade teacher extraordinaire and for me, one important answer is that a unit of study on poetry can teach children to explore, and savor language, valuing voice and repetition, sounds and onomatopoeia (even if they never hear any of these terms). They can learn to read and to write with an ear, appreciating and revising the pace and rhythm of words, and they can learn to care not only about their topics, but also about *how they write* about those topics. Poetry can teach children to deliberately craft their language, trying things on the page on purpose, hoping to create special effects.

Poetry can also encourage young children to see the world with fresh eyes. A plane flies overhead, leaving a trail of white. "That plane just left a scar in the sky," my son Miles observed. Miles wasn't *trying* to use figurative language, nor did he rely on a knowledge of simile and metaphor. He simply said what he saw. Children can learn to see with their hearts, to show their feelings by capering and pretending and imagining with language. They can learn to have fun with words, to be daredevils and gymnasts with language.

About the Unit

Long before this study formally began, Stephanie started to listen to the way her students spoke and to notice and celebrate the poems in their everyday speech. When Maddie said, "Now that Mommy works again, I do my own ponytail. Daddy tried but it was all wrong!" Stephanie wrote Maddie's words up on a chart for shared reading. When Daniel said, "Did you know that squirrels plant more trees than humans? They forget where they buried their food and . . . a little rain, a little sun . . . then BOOM! A tree!" Stephanie gave everyone copies and arranged a choral reading of Daniel's poem.

For Stephanie's first graders, every day's morning meeting began with a poem. Often Stephanie would simply say, "I found a poem that's perfect for today. Let me read it to you." Then she'd read it, usually more than once, leaving a halo of silence around the words. Other days, Stephanie and her children would revisit a familiar poem in order to do choral or dramatic readings of it. A few poems became such a part of life in their classroom that at any point in the day, Stephanie or a child could start chanting the poem and others would join in. Once, in line on

the playground, Stephanie started her children off with Eloise Greenfield's "Way Down in the Music":

> I get way down in the music
> Down inside the music
> I let it wake me
> take me
> Spin me around and make me
> Uh-get down[1]

Soon a few of her youngsters were slapping imaginary bongo drums on their thighs, a few had created a chorus out of uh-huh, uh-huhs . . . and while standing in line on the tarmac, the class had orchestrated a choral performance of the poem.

Her children knew and loved Beatrice Schenk de Regniers' "Keep a Poem in Your Pocket." It, too, was deep in their bones, and sometimes they'd recite the opening verse:

> Keep a poem in your pocket
> And a picture in your head
> And you'll never feel lonely
> At night when you're in bed.[2]

The class had found a way to put "April Rain Song," by Langston Hughes, to music, using xylophones to re-create the sound and feel of gentle showers. All these are ways to help your students get ready for a unit of study on poetry.

---

[1] In *Honey I Love and Other Poems* by Eloise Greenfield, (Harper Trophy, 1978)
[2] In *Something Special* by Beatrice Schenk de Regniers (Harcourt, 1958)

SEEING WITH POETS' EYES

GETTING READY

- Special new poetry folders (or cleaned-out old folders) to mark this momentous occasion
- Observation paper (not poetry paper), with room for both pictures and words (you may also want to give each child a clipboard if you have enough)
- Objects, arranged in a "poetry museum," chosen to teach youngsters to observe carefully and to see with poets' eyes (in one area, you might display a few carefully chosen shells; in another, a piece of driftwood or a lovely leaf or some special rocks); you'll soon invite children to add their own objects to this poetry museum
- "Pencil Sharpener," "Ceiling," and other poems of your choice, written on chart paper
- Copy of Byrd Baylor's *The Other Way to Listen*

THE FIRST DAY OF ANY NEW UNIT *should begin with a generous invitation. We imagined a host of ways to issue such an invitation. We could invite children to read, reread, set to music, and perform a few poems so those poems got into their bones. Or we could help children study a single poem closely, collecting their observations about the genre. In the end, our first priority was to create a context in which poetry would grow. We wanted our room to invite children to give respectful, reverent attention to the details of our lives. Saul Bellow, a Nobel Laureate of literature, says that to write, we must connect with our "observing instrument":*

> *There is that observing instrument in us—in childhood, at any rate—at the sight of a man's face, his shoes, the color of light. . . . From this source come words, phrases, syllables.*

We decided to launch this unit by teaching children to use all their senses, plus their hearts and minds and imaginations, to take in the details of their lives in fresh ways. We'd do this by creating a museum of objects in the classroom and inviting children to marvel at the mysteries of these objects, as suggested by the poet Patricia Hubbell:

> *When I was ten years old, I started a museum in the playhouse in our backyard. I filled the shelves with birds' nests, rocks, shells, pressed wildflowers. . . . About the time I started the museum, I began to write poems. . . . I wrote about the things in my museum. Birds' nests and rocks, leaves and butterflies found their way into the poems.*

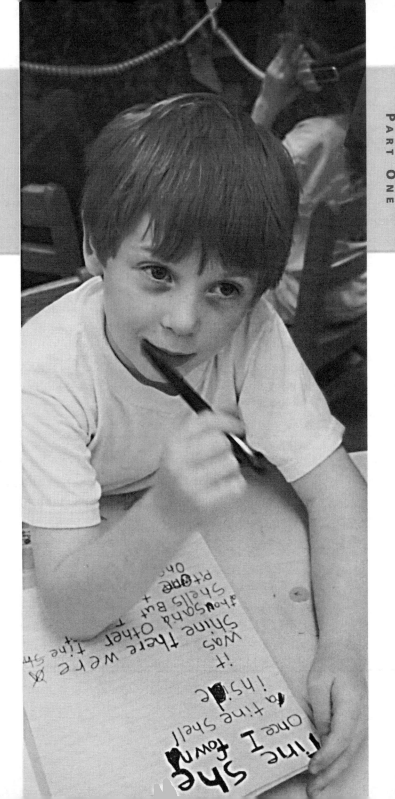

THE MINILESSON

Connection

Celebrate the way the class has immersed itself in poetry, and tell children that today you'll teach them to see the world in fresh ways, like poets do.

"Writers, today is an important day. We have been reading lots of poems together all year, and poems have been sprouting up all over our classroom—on our walls and windows and doors. Our room has been getting ready for us to be poets! Today we are going to learn how poets see the world in different, fresh, and unusual ways. Then we are going to see the world like poets."

Teach

Tell the children you'll show them how one poet saw an object in a fresh new way. Tell them the poet could have seen and described the object in regular words but instead saw the object with a poet's eyes.

"So, poets, I've brought some poems written by your favorite poet—Zoë! Today let's pay special attention to how Zoë sees the world in a fresh new way. In this poem, Zoë writes about a pencil sharpener. Look at the pencil sharpener." Stephanie looked intently at it and paused. "What I see is a gray box, a machine, that makes my pencil sharp." Stephanie's intonation suggested this was a bland way to see.

"But I'm going to read a poem Zoë wrote about the pencil sharpener, and you will see what I mean about how poets see things in fresh new ways." Stephanie read "Pencil Sharpener," which she had written on chart paper and displayed on an easel.

Stephanie and I use more figurative language and speak in more poetic ways during poetry minilessons than we do in other minilessons. We're trying to create a context in which poetry will grow, and in part we do this by immersing children in fresh, precise language. In this first minilesson Stephanie invites children into the world of poetry so they'll assume the identities of poets.

I often help children understand what I'm talking about by describing also what I'm not talking about. Here, Stephanie and I want children to notice that poets see even something as ordinary as a pencil sharpener in fresh ways. To highlight what we mean, Stephanie paints a contrast.

Pencil Sharpener
by Zoë Ryder White

I think there are a hundred bees
inside the pencil sharpener
and they buzz
and buzz
and buzz
until my point
is sharp!

Highlight the novelty in the poet's vision by reminding children that the poet could have seen and described the object in another—drabber—way.

"Poets, when I read this poem, I was so surprised! I don't usually think about our pencil sharpener like Zoë describes it! I usually think of it as just a machine that makes my pencil sharp. But Zoë sees the pencil sharpener like a poet sees it, in a fresh new way! She imagines that there are *bees* inside the pencil sharpener and that they are buzzing around the tip of her pencil to make it sharp! Imagine that! This poem makes *me* see our classroom pencil sharpener in a fresh new way, and that's what poetry can do."

Active Engagement

Ask the children to think how they would write with poets' eyes about another object—then show what the poet did.

"Zoë wrote another poem, this one about the ceiling. Would you try looking at our ceiling right now? Look with a poet's eyes and see it in a fresh new way." Stephanie looked intently at the ceiling. "Tell your partner what you see when you look at the ceiling with a poet's eyes." Immediately the room filled with talk. "Okay, let's read Zoë's poem and pay special attention to the fresh new way she saw the ceiling." As Stephanie read "Ceiling" to the class, the children followed along, because it, too, had been written on chart paper.

"Poets, what did you notice about how Zoë saw the ceiling?"
Marco: "She saw the ceiling as a sky!"
Aja: "She probably pretended the lights were the sun."
"I know, poets, that you all saw the ceiling in other fresh, new ways, and maybe during this unit some of you will decide to write about our ceiling, or about other parts of our classroom."

Stephanie begins this minilesson by telling the children what she's going to do—read a poem—and what it is she wants them to listen for—she hopes they notice how Zoë, a teacher-poet and friend to the class, sees the pencil sharpener in a new way.

The poem is a very sparse one, written for the purpose of this minilesson. It is especially effective because it doesn't rely on a dozen poetic devices in order to work. The most striking feature of the poem is the one that Stephanie and I have decided to highlight.

Stephanie is mentoring her children in the process of learning from a poet. The truth is that Stephanie can see the poetry in a pencil sharpener more than she lets on. . . . but she says, "that just looks like a grey box to me" because she knows that's what many of her children see, and she wants to demonstrate what it can mean to let a poet surprise and inform us.

Ceiling
by Zoë Ryder White

The ceiling
is the sky
for the classroom.

We selected this very simple, brief poem, as we selected "Pencil Sharpener," because these are models to which children can aspire and because the dominant feature of both poems is the one we're trying to highlight. In longer, lusher poems, the poet will have done so many things that the poems won't illustrate our point—that poets see the world with fresh new eyes—as well.

Confirm the wise comments your children make. Restate the bigger point that poets see in fresh new ways.

"In poems, we see the world in ways we never imagined before. We look at the world closely and carefully; we look with our hearts and our minds. We try to let an ordinary ol' ceiling matter to us. And now, because of this poem, we get to think of our regular ol' ceiling as a sky, a sky that goes on and on."

Link

Send kids off to study objects you've brought (feathers, shells) and to see them in fresh new ways.

"Today is an exciting day, poets, because today you are going to practice seeing the world with poets' eyes. You'll try to see in fresh new ways! At each of your tables, you will find brand-new poetry folders, and these contain special clipboards and paper for recording what you see (like we recorded in science the other day). We won't start writing poems until tomorrow. For now, find an interesting thing to look at and write what you see."

"After this, for the rest of your life, whenever you want to write a poem, remember that you need to see the world with a poet's eyes. Stretch your imagination and look in ways that are brand new! You don't want to just write, 'The pine cone is brown.' Instead you might write, 'The pine cone is a wooden porcupine' or 'The pine cone is a tree for an elf.'"

"We're going to start off today at our own tables, but each table has something different to look at, so when you have sketched and described what's at your table, you can decide to go to another table. Green table, get started."

You will have heard some of the children's observations as they talked with their partners, so you can draw out comments you especially like. Don't elicit more than a few suggestions because your time is limited.

"A sky that goes on and on" is a nice embellishment. Stephanie is demonstrating that a poem helps create images in her mind, but she doesn't make a fuss about this. She knows a good minilesson usually makes a single teaching point.

Usually we don't send children off with instructions to spend the entire writing workshop doing what we assign. Instead, minilessons usually end with us reminding children to add what we've taught to their repertoire, and meanwhile, to continue their ongoing work. Today's send off is different from usual.

We're setting children up to observe with poets' eyes and jot down observations. We've not yet asking them to write poems because we couldn't find a way to address both the vision and fresh language and also the line breaks and form of poetry both in one minilesson. The clipboard observations allow us to teach a second minilesson before children draft poems.

You may want to push children to attend to a single object for a longer stretch of time. "We'll study one object for twenty minutes (that's a very long time), then we'll rotate the objects." In courses for professional writers, one might spend a day describing an egg in its shell or an eggplant. To write well, we must learn to look long and close and to notice what others would pass by.

MID-WORKSHOP TEACHING POINT

Point out that although the children are looking for a long while at one object, they're frantically rushing from one lens to another. Remind children to slow down.

"Poets, can I stop you for a minute? What I'm noticing is that many of you are looking at your object in one way, then in another way, then in yet another way. So you are saying, 'The leaf is like a little fan.' And then you go to a totally *different* way of seeing and say, 'The leaf is like grass, smashed together.' Then you try yet *another* way of looking and say, 'The leaf is sort of like a little tree.' What I want to tell you is *slow down*. If you say the leaf is like a little tree, look again at the leaf. How is it like a little tree? Do the veins, the little lines, look like branches? How can you describe the color of green in that leaf? Look really closely at the stem. Don't jump so quickly from seeing it one way to seeing it another way, okay?"

MORE MID-WORKSHOP TEACHING POINT

Intervene to read aloud an excerpt from Byrd Baylor's *The Other Way to Listen*.

"Poets, I want to read you a little bit of a book about seeing and hearing like a poet. I'll be reading from *The Other Way to Listen*, by Byrd Baylor and Peter Parnall. Listen closely; this is my very favorite picture book in the world. The book tells of lessons the narrator learns from a wise old man."

"When the narrator asks the old man to teach her to hear a sky full of stars or a cactus blooming in the dark, the wise old man says, "'Most people never near those things at all.'"

"The narrator is insistent. 'Just give me a clue on how to start,' she pleads."

"And that is what we're doing today." Stephanie read an excerpt from the book that describes a wise old man's advice to get to know one thing very well.

The secret to rigorous teaching is that after you issue an invitation (as Stephanie did in this minilesson), you need to study what your students do, asking, "How can I intervene to lift the level of this work?" To know ways to help, we need to teach on our toes, expecting children to need coaching in ways that surprise us. How crucial it is to look honestly at what your children are actually doing and to believe your teaching can address issues you see. This particular intervention may not be exactly right for your youngsters, but the fact that we intervene to address issues we see is crucial.

TIME TO CONFER

Early in a unit of study, use your conferences to recruit children into an energetic involvement in the new work. This means your early conferences will be especially closely linked to the minilesson. Across many different units of study, your early-in-the-unit conferences will probably work toward these goals:

- Generate social energy and enthusiasm for the new topic. "That's so cool—show Ramon what you did. Maybe he could join you and then you could teach the class!" In this session specifically, get clusters of children excited about looking with poets' eyes.
- Help a few children find special success in a particular unit. Give a few selected children a brief piggyback ride early on in the unit so that, with the help of very strong scaffolding, lo and behold, they find that they are doing exemplary work. Specifically, this might mean that while most of your children are still writing their observations, you may want to help a few get started writing not only observations but also poems. You can use what these few children produce as models when you teach the next day. See the conference cited at right from the *Conferring with Primary Writers* book. They may not have gotten to this place independently, but you can nevertheless help them build a new image of themselves around the fact that they are doing magnificent work.

These conferences in *The Conferring Handbook* may be especially helpful today:

- *"Can You Think of One Moment That Holds the Big Feeling the Ocean Gives You?"*
- *"Are Those the Sounds You Hear?"*
- *"Can You Help Me See What You Saw?"*

Also, if you have *Conferring with Primary Writers*, you may want to refer to the following conference:

- "Can I Help You Come Up with Ideas?"

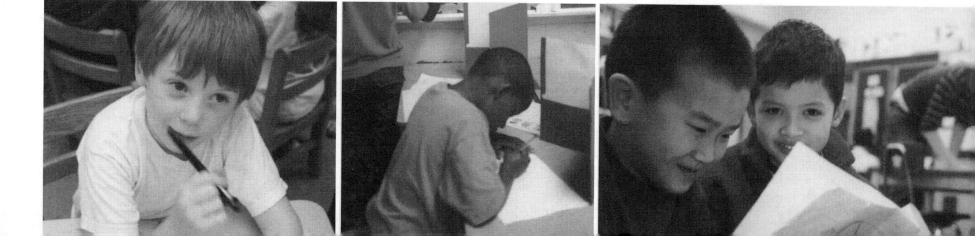

After-the-Workshop Share

Celebrate the ways the children looked with fresh eyes by citing bits they've written.

"What an exciting day! I heard so many amazing ways to look at the world coming out of your poetry pencils today! Toby wrote that the shell was a tiny pink ear! And Ronia wrote that the piece of wood was a sailboat for a mouse! You are really seeing the world like poets do. Would you share what you wrote—and saw—with your partner?"

Stephanie pulled up a chair to listen to two partners. Daniel had described a shell this way: "It looks like the sunset. It smells like grapes." Sarah had written about a rock. [*Fig. I-1*]

Tell the children that poets also look at ordinary things with fresh eyes, and ask them to do so with one of their shoes.

"Did you know that poets look at the most ordinary things in their world in this new way? They don't just look at *special* things—they look at ordinary things too. That is the real magic of poetry. Poets look at chairs and tables and floor tiles—and their own shoes with poets' eyes. In fact, let's all try this right this minute. Look at your very own shoe, right there on your very own foot. What do you see? Think in your mind for a minute about this." Stephanie waited for a moment. "Turn and tell your partner what you see when you look at your shoe with a poet's eyes. After all, you are looking at the shoe of a poet!"

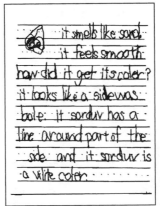

It smells like sand.
It feels smooth.
How did it get its color?
It looks like a sideways bowl.
It sort of has a line around part of the side and it sort of is a velvet color.

Fig. I-1   Sarah

This is a perfect share because it supports what children have done and lifts their work one tiny step. Also, every child is actively involved! This could, of course, also have been the next minilesson. Often the different components of a session are interchangeable.

Revisit this topic after Session V. By then your children will have chosen their own topics and you won't be extending the time kids write about objects you set out in the poetry museum.

▸ If many of your children wrote observations that more closely resemble those of a scientist than a poet, tell children, "Your notes seem more like a scientist's notes than a poet's." You could show children the differences.

Scientist's Notes on a Leaf	Poet's Notes on a Leaf
One inch long, three inches wide	Tiny enough to be a tree for a village of snails
Sawtooth edges	It's as if someone scissored the edges to make
Dark green on one side	them pretty
Paler green on other side	And painted on a deep forest green
Veins stick out	

After children study the differences, ask the class to see an object you select (perhaps a window pane, a cloud in the sky) with scientists' eyes and then to with poets' eyes.

▸ You could do the same lesson using a safety pin. After saying what a scientist might see when she looked at a safety pin, you could tell the children to notice next what a poet sees when studying the same safety pin. Read Valerie Worth's poem "Safety Pin," in which she likens an opened safety pin to a small silver fish.

▸ Teach children to look closely and draw with detail. The poet Karla Kuskin once said, "If you are going to draw, you have to look at that leaf and see the way the lines come down. You have to see the way the leaf is shaped and the way each plant grows differently. When you're drawing, you're drawing details and that's what you're writing about, too."

▸ You could suggest that the class sit under the tree, or visit the school library, or sit on the front steps of the school and that they do these things like poets, really seeing and hearing and noticing.

Safety Pin
by Valerie Worth

Closed, it sleeps
On its side
Quietly,
The silver
Image
Of some
Small fish;

Opened, it snaps
Its tail out
Like a thin
Shrimp, and looks
At the sharp
Point with a
Surprised eye.

The focus of our teaching in this first lesson has been on helping children see and use language in fresh ways. As you look over your children's work after this first session, pay special attention to the way they're using language. Sometimes children seem to stumble on a beautiful way of saying something, and you'll want to be there when this happens (or as soon afterward as possible), ready to celebrate what the child has done. When you take children's work home, therefore, your first goal will be to search for treasures. You—like your kids—will be working on finding miracles in the mundane! Just as a leaf can, at first glance, look ordinary, so too can your children's work, at first glance, look ordinary. Train yourself to see!

When you see that one child has done a particular thing well, search for a second example of the same type of thing. Once you find several examples of, say, sensory details or of surprising language, you have the ingredients you need to make a powerful teaching point.

Meanwhile, try to discern your children's image of poetry. What is it they are trying to do when they write poems? You'll want to teach in a way which lifts and informs their image of poetry.

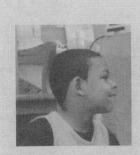

LISTENING FOR LINE BREAKS

GETTING READY

▶ Poetry paper
▶ Rebecca's poem, written on chart paper as prose
▶ Chunks of Rebecca's poem written on sentence strips or word cards
▶ Pocket chart on which the sentence strips or word cards can be arranged and displayed
● See CD-ROM for resources

YOUR CHILDREN HAVE NOW JOTTED *observational notes about small treasures (a feather, a stone), but they have yet to turn those notes into poems. Today you highlight a second, hugely important feature of poetry— that line breaks influence the sound of poems—and then launch your children into spinning the flax of observational notes into the golden threads of poetry.*

One way to highlight line breaks is to ask children to reread a published poem with the eyes of someone who is about to make the same kind of thing. During the Nonfiction unit of study, your children learned that when they want to try a new kind of writing, it can help to look at the work of another author and notice the features of that work. They should be good at doing this by now. You can probably count on their noticing the format, specifically, the line breaks of poems.

Your goal today is also to teach children to craft and revise written language in an effort to convey meaning. You'll want to show that poets work hard to make their poems "sound right." Poets have strategies for influencing the sound of their poems (line breaks, repetition, alliteration, assonance), and eventually your children will explore these strategies. Today, you will simply put sound out there as one of the big concerns for every poet.

By the end of today's minilesson, students should be ready to go back to their observational notes, drafting them into poems (if they weren't written that way from the start) and experimenting with the format. You hope they'll write their content one way, then another, asking, "Does this way of laying my words on the page match what I'm trying to say?"

THE MINILESSON

Connection

Tell the children that you're amazed at their fresh ways of seeing the world and want to teach a second ingredient in poetry—music. Give examples of the good work they've done.

"Kids, I have to tell you, I am amazed by some of the fresh new ways you are looking at the world. Just a few minutes ago, Hana told me that leaves are like a birthday cake to a slug! Did any of you ever think of a leaf that way? I know I didn't."

"So it seems to me that you are ready to think about really making poems. You know how cakes have ingredients? Well, poems have ingredients, too. We already learned about one ingredient: to make a poem you need to look with a poet's eyes at ordinary things. But today I want to teach you that there is a second ingredient. To make a poem you also need music. Poems have their own special *music*."

"We don't usually sing or play instruments to give poems music. No, the music of poems comes from how the words of a poem are chosen and how they are put onto the paper. Poets try to write words on the paper in such a way that readers will read our poems with music. Today I want to teach you that one way to give our poems music is to divide our words into lines that go down the paper." As I spoke about lining going down the paper in a column-like fashion, I showed the layout of poems with my hands.

You may be thinking, "My children would never say something like Hana said." But you can make these jewels happen. If one of your children looked at the snail and said, "That guy loves to eat!" you could respond, "The leaves are probably like a . . . a . . . dessert to the slug." "Yeah," the child will probably add something like, "The leaves are like ice cream. The leaves are like a birthday cake." Later, you repeat what the child said without mentioning that you coauthored the metaphor.

This minilesson is ambitious. Your children won't entirely grasp these concepts, but a minilesson, like a piece of literature, can inspire and uplift even if it's not totally concrete in a child's mind. Stephanie and I have certainly laid out two of the primary tensions poets work with when they compose poetry: language and sound.

We've downplayed (for now) the third crucial dimension: meaning. By putting little objects about the room and telling children to write about those things, we have taken topic choice away. But the role of meaning will be dealt with soon.

Teach

Ask the children to study a poem that you'll have copied without line breaks. Read the poem aloud in a blah, prose-like way to suggest that this definitely doesn't work.

"Let's take a closer look at the poem we have taped to our fish tank, "Aquarium," by Valerie Worth. I've written it two different ways up here on chart paper. One way does not give the poem music, and the other way does."

I read aloud the poem I had written on chart paper as prose, without line breaks:

> Goldfish flash gold and silver scales; they flick and slip away under green
> weed—But round brown snails stick to the glass and stay.

"When I write the poem out in this way, the layout on the page tells me to read it just like I'm talking to you. Because all the words go across the page, I read this like I'm telling you I went to the store and bought some gum, or something. It's kind of like blah, blah, blah. There's really not much music here."

Contrast this by showing and reading the same poem written with the line breaks the author intended. Discuss why the line breaks support the meaning and influence your reading.

"Now, on the other hand, look at this version!" I flipped the chart paper to reveal the next page, where I'd written the poem as Valerie Worth intended, with line breaks. I read aloud the first five lines only, then paused to discuss it.

The poem, without line breaks and music:	Valerie Worth's version:
Goldfish flash gold and silver scales; they flick and slip away under green weed—But round brown snails stick to the glass and stay.	Goldfish Flash Gold and silver scales; They flick and slip away Under green weed— But round brown snails Stick To the glass And stay.

When we study a text within a minilesson, it is almost always a familiar text. This poem was already taped on the aquarium. I wrote the new, prose-like version of Valerie's poem on chart paper for the purpose of today's minilesson.

The brevity of this poem is intentional. In every minilesson, I am always thinking about ways to make my point in less time.

I read only half the poem aloud because in a minute I will invite all the kids to read the whole thing aloud, and I want to leave some of the fun for them. It is common for the teacher to do half of something during the teaching component of a minilesson and then turn the work over to children to complete during the active involvement component of the minilesson.

"When I read the poem *with* line breaks, it sounds different, doesn't it? When Valerie Worth divided the words into lines, she sort of 'told me' to read the poem in a certain way. She is trying to make me read it so my voice moves like a fish swims." I moved my hand down the print, snaking my hand about as a fish would swerve through the water. "All these words are in a fishlike line down the page, and the lines go back and forth, flicking this way and flicking that way. In this line [four], when she wrote, 'They flick and slip away,' I think she decided to put those words on one line to show that in one instant, the fish are there *and* gone. By the next line, all we see is green weed, and under it—snails."

Active Engagement

Ask the children to read the poem aloud, using line breaks as the author instructed them to do.

"Try reading the first part—the fast, flitty-fish part—of the poem to your partner, and then read this slow, snail part." As I pointed to the top and the bottom halves of the poem, I let my voice change from a flighty fish to a slow snail. "Notice how Valerie Worth makes you read the snail part differently."

The room erupted with voices reading and then discussing. After two minutes, I intervened. "I heard many of you read it like this." I read the first four lines in a light, quick, flitting way. Then I switched my voice to match the slow snails on the bottom of the aquarium.

When I have something to say to children, I don't hesitate to do so. I'm free to tell children what I notice about the line breaks of Worth's poem. If I tried to extract these same observations from the class, it would have taken me exponentially longer to make my point, and the lesson could easily have been buried in a lot of convoluted questioning. On the other hand, I do need to worry whether children are really listening to and "getting" what I try to teach. I use the visual support of the written poem and my gestures, plus an expressive voice and eye contact, to make it likely that they are mentally with me.

The way I give instructions provides the children with a lot of guidance!

In an instance like this, I don't check that every child has completed the task before I reconvene the group. It doesn't really matter to me if they have completed the task. If they've given this a quick try, they'll be more ready to learn from me.

Goldfish
by Valerie Worth

Flash
Gold and silver scales;
They flick and slip away
Under green weed—
But round brown snails
Stick
To the glass
And stay.

Summarize what you want the children to learn.

"What I want you to notice is that Valerie Worth—like every poet—uses line breaks to help her readers turn her poem into music. She uses line breaks to help us read her words like fast fish and like slow snails."

Tell the children about a child who wants help with line breaks. Recruit your children's help.

"Yesterday a poet from last year's class came by with a poem and wanted help with line breaks. Stephanie and I are meeting her at lunch to give her some ideas, but we thought you all might help. Let me read her poem for you, and see if you can make some line break suggestions."

I revealed a piece of chart paper on which Rebecca's poem was written like prose. Beside this, Stephanie and I had a blue plastic pocket chart we sometimes used during shared reading. Each word of the poem was on a word card.

Fireworks cracking the sky. Big balls of fire bursting into bloom and fading upon the dark lonely sky.

"Will you and your partner do (in your mind) with Rebecca's poem what you'll soon do with your own poems? Read the poem over a few times, then talk about what it really means and how the words could be laid out on the page to match the meaning."

You could stop your minilesson here. Stephanie and I press on because we want to rally her children to care about line breaks and show them that writers experiment with line breaks to figure out how a poem "should go." Our ambitious goals mean we have double-decker active involvement in this minilesson.

The "exercise text" is very, very brief. This matters. Notice also that we continually stress that a poet tries to make line breaks support the meaning of the poem.

We considered asking children to rewrite the poem on their whiteboards, but this would take time. We could also have passed out envelopes containing little word cards and asked partners to lay these out on the rug. We decided to go for the simpler idea of just asking them to point and talk.

Ask one child to show the class how he might lay out the words and lines of this poem.

Soon Raymond was at the front of the room, slotting word cards into plastic pockets to create his version of the poem:

Fireworks
Cracking the
Sky
Big balls of fire
Bursting forth into bloom
And
Fading

Upon

The dark
Lonely

Sky.

"Do you see how Raymond made his poem match the fireworks with big splashes of color that happen once, soon again, and then fade away? And the sky," I pointed to that word card, "really is lonely here by itself. So there are lots of possible ways to lay out our words. The main thing is that we make them match the meaning of the poem. That's beautiful!"

"How many of you imagined different ways this could go? Thumbs up. Great!"

You won't want to invest time in having child after child show their plan for line breaks. You can make your point with a single example.

Again, I compliment the line breaks because "they match the meaning."

Having celebrated one way to lay out a poem, it's wise to also give a nod to the many other solutions children have invented.

Link

Remind the children they have options, including the option to observe with poets' eyes, to turn notes into poems, or to rewrite poems with line breaks.

"Today, poets, will you go back to your centers and to your precious objects? You can continue seeing with a poet's eyes and collecting notes. Or you can take the notes you wrote yesterday and start turning these into poems with line breaks. You'll probably write those one way, then another. After this, any day when you write poems, remember that we're trying to turn words into music—and line breaks can help us do that."

MID-WORKSHOP TEACHING POINT

Show how one child wrote his poem in several different ways. Ask partners to imagine how they could write their poems differently.

"Poets, can I stop all of you? I want to tell you about the brilliant work Zach is doing. Zach is turning his notes about a leaf into a poem. First he reread his notes and crossed out 'the boring parts' (that's the way he put it), and then he looked again with a poet's eyes, finding more to say about his leaf. Then he took his words and ideas and wrote them one way on the page—see, look." Stephanie held one version up. "Then he said, 'Wait a minute. Hmm . . .' *and he wrote them another way*! So far he has written about this one leaf three different ways! That is exactly what poets do."

"Would you all get with your partner and talk over how else you could write *your* poem? Talk not only about how it might go but also about *why* it might go that way. Okay?" After five minutes, I ended the conversations and asked the children to resume their writing.

Our minilessons and conferences usually end with us extrapolating the larger lesson we hope writers will carry with them to other days and other texts. That is, we make an effort to explicitly teach toward tomorrow as well as today. "After this, any day when you write poems. . . ." we say. Also, in our minilessons (more so than in conferences) we try to leave children aware of their options. We are trying to expand children's repertoire of strategies rather than assign a particular strategy to all children.

When possible, it helps to teach children strategies and goals. This minilesson taught the goal (poems that are laid out on the page in a pattern that supports the meaning of the poem), and this mid-workshop advice equips children with one strategy for accomplishing this goal (writing the same text in different ways).

Notice the tiny bits of added rigor that are tucked in, as when I say, "Talk not only about how it might go but also about why it might go that way."

TIME TO CONFER

Now that you've invited children to write poems, you can be sure that some children will produce "Roses are red, violets are blue" ditties. Although you won't have mentioned rhyme, some of them will forsake the idea that poets begin by looking closely in order to rhyme. You have lots of options for how to respond:

- You could conduct a quality-of-good-writing conference. Try to learn more about what she's aiming for when she writes a poem. Tell her what you are coming to understand: "So am I right that you mainly try to make your poems rhyme? Do you think 'the cat/sat/on a mat/' would be a great poem?" Then be explicit about your hopes to expand or change the child's goals. Perhaps say, "I think little kids think that way, but I want to teach you that real poets not only want their poems to sound in certain ways, they also want to say something important. Let's look again at this acorn and think about what you could say about it that feels important."
- You could use a content conference such as those at right. Act as if the child's got an early draft down and focus now on *the subject,* luring her to do the same. "'I have a dog/She eats like a hog. . . .' I never knew you even *had* a cat! Tell me about her. Can you picture her? Tell me what you see exactly—say only true words." After transcribing selected bits of what the child says, you can say, "Can I read you what you've written? Your poem is getting *so* much better! It has true details in it now, and I can picture it."

These conferences in *The Conferring Handbook* may be especially helpful today:

- *"Can You Think of One Moment That Holds the Big Feeling the Ocean Gives You?"*
- *"Are Those the Sounds You Hear?"*
- *"Can You Help Me See What You Saw?"*

Also, if you have *Conferring with Primary Writers,* you may want to refer to the conferences in part seven.

Show a poem a child wrote in which the child experimented with line breaks. Ask partners to talk about what the child changed between one version and another, and why he may have made the changes.

"Writers, I need to show you something very smart that Alex did. He'd been writing about the photograph of trees we have in our museum, and he started to write a poem about trees in winter. He read what he'd written over and over and realized that to make it sound right, he needed not only to lay it out right on the page, but also to add some words! Look at his first version." I pointed to a chart-paper copy of Alex's poem.

Taping a second version alongside the first, I said, "Now look at his next version. Listen as I read it aloud. Tell your partner what he changed, and why he might have done this."

First Version	Second Version
Winter	Winter
In the winter	In the
The trees have no	Cold
Fingers	Lonely
	Winter
	The trees
	Have
	No
	Fingers

Ask the children to talk with their partners about what they've done and how Alex's work could nudge them to make new revisions.

"Now, would you look with your partner at *your* poems to see if Alex's work gives you ideas for revising your poems?"

Consider doing some extension minilessons after Session VI. By then children will be well launched into poems on topics of their own choosing.

▶ Choose a poem in which the line breaks clearly support the meaning. Write it in several formats. Ask children to tell you which way they believe the author selected and to talk about why that way best supports the poem's meaning. (See "Poem" and "Rain into River.") Instead of using published poems, you could use a "poem" that consists of the word *drip* written on eight word cards, *drop* written on eight word cards and *sunshine* written on three word cards. Ask, "If this were a poem named 'Sudden Storm,' how might it go? If it were named 'Spring Showers,' how might it go?" A child could lay these words out on a pocket chart trying to let their layout echo the poem's meaning.

▶ Words are arranged on the page in units that create sounds and silences. It's important that children not only *listen* to poems read aloud but that they also *read* poems aloud. Teach them to read aloud respecting the line breaks and white space that call for bits of silence. Tell them to let the words create images and to listen for rhyme and the repetition, knowing these glue the parts of the poem into a whole.

▶ Invite them to search for poems hiding in picture books. Alternatively, show them a very poetic book, like Cynthia Rylant's *Night in the Country*. Read a few pages of it aloud, show the pages to the children, and ask, "How else could she have laid out the words and page breaks? Why did she do it this way?"

Poem
by William Carlos Williams

As the cat
climbed over
the top of

the jamcloset
first the right
forefoot

carefully
then the hind
stepped down

into the pit of
the empty
flower pot.

Rain into River
by X.J. Kennedy

Rain into river
falling

tingles

one
at
a
time

the trout's
tin shingles.

HEARING THE MUSIC IN POETRY

GETTING READY

▶ Small copy of a poem you love (perhaps "Things," by Eloise Greenfield) folded up, in your wallet

▶ Same poem, written twice on chart paper, once correctly and then as a possible earlier draft

▶ Several kinds of poetry paper in the writing center (the paper will probably be long and thin)

○ See CD-ROM for resources

IN THIS SESSION, YOU ENCOURAGE CHILDREN to think about the sounds of language as they write poems. Try to convey that writers select their words and lay them on the page in deliberate ways that will influence how readers read those poems. Although you will eventually teach specific strategies for making poems sound good (like repetition and alliteration), in this session aim toward the broader goal of teaching children to reread their poems-under-construction often, shifting between writing and reading as they draft. Your hope is that if children read their poems aloud with reverence and with attentiveness to meaning, this will elevate their sense of what it is they are doing.

Remember that, for now, children are still generating poems or revising poems in response to little treasures you've put out. Soon you'll challenge them to do all this work while selecting topics they care about.

For today, you'll say, "Reread your drafts often. Make your voice support the meaning in the poem." Then you'll send them off to alternate between writing and reading, working along to bring out a song in their poems.

The Minilesson

Connection

Tell a story of a poem that has been sung to you or to someone you know, and use this story to tell the children that poetry is close to music.

> "When I was little, my dad used to dry me off by rubbing a towel like this: back and forth, back and forth. While he did it, he'd sing me a song, 'Skiddley dinky dinky do, I love you. I love you in the morning and in the afternoon. I love you in the sunshine and in the rainstorms too. Skiddley dinky dinky do, I love you.'"

> "It was sort of like that song in Robert Munsch's book *Love You Forever*. Remember it? 'I'll love you forever, I like you for always, as long as you're living, my baby you'll be.'"

> "I'm telling you this because I think poems are very close to music. Today I want to teach you how important it is for poets like you to read and reread and reread poems until they sound *just right*. We'll do this with published poems, then with our own poems. Always, like any poet, we'll listen for the songs our poems are trying to sing."

Substitute your own anecdotes. Children love hearing personal, true stories about the role poetry has played in your life. Did your mother use to chide, "Sarah, Sarah, strong and able. Keep your elbows off the table?" If so, use that poem as your example. Did you and your friends use poems as jump-rope jingles? If your childhood was devoid of poetry, you can either pretend otherwise, or you can tell the story, in today's minilesson, of a writer-friend named Lucy whose father used to sing a song that went, "Skiddley dinky dinky do. . . ."

Teach

Share a poem that you always carry with you. Tell the children that when you love a poem, you reread it until you can hear the song. Read it once in a robotic way and another time beautifully.

> "I have a poem I carry with me always. I keep it in my wallet and reread it often." I took Eloise Greenfield's "Things" out of the photo section of my wallet and unfolded it while the children watched. "The first time I ever read 'Things' I was just getting the words straight. It didn't sound like a poem at all! I read it like this." I read a portion of it in a choppy, robotic way.

Okay, okay. So this might be stretching things a bit! Maybe this poem just got into my wallet a day ago. I have no problem exaggerating my love of literacy so that I make my point!

"Then I reread the poem, and *this* time I *really* paid attention to what the words were saying. Like here," I pointed to the first *Ain't got it no more*, "I thought, 'That's sad—the candy's all gone.' And I reread it with that feeling in my voice. I tried to think and feel what the words were saying."

"I also tried to take a little breath after each line because I know Eloise wrote the lines this way so readers would take little breaths before going on to new lines."

"When I read this poem now, it's like a song to me. Listen." I read the poem again. After reading it this time with rhythm, feeling and respect for line breaks, I said, "That was better! Next, I decided to make myself some notes so I would remember how to read it really well. I wanted to remember that when I read *beach*, I want to make a picture in my mind of a long, white stretch of sand. So I wrote *Picture it* on a sticky note and put it beside the word *beach*. I decided that I needed to slow down for the last two lines, "Still got it / Still got it." Those two lines are so important. So I wrote *Slow* on another sticky note."
As I spoke, I reenacted how I'd written sticky notes and put them into the poem.

Tell the children that when writing as well as when reading poems, you reread and try to hear the song. Suggest and reenact how the poet—in this case, Eloise Greenfield— probably did this.

"I write poems by putting some words on the page, then reading what I've written, to hear the song in the words. Then I fix up the words so they sound better, and write some more words, and I reread again. Eloise might have had a draft that went like this" I said, and showed them my imagined versions of her drafts.

went to the beach
played on the shore
built me a sand house
ain't got it no more
walked to the corner store
bought me some soda and candy
ain't got it no more.

You could no doubt talk at some length about the decisions you made as you tried to read the poem aloud well. Don't go on and on. These two particulars are enough to give children the general idea that you focus on meaning when you try to read it well.

Things
by Eloise Greenfield

Went to the corner
Walked in the store
Bought me some candy
Ain't got it no more
Ain't got it no more

Went to the beach
Played on the shore
Built me a sand house
Ain't got it no more
Ain't got it no more

Went to the kitchen
Lay down on the floor
Made me a poem
Still got it
Still got it

"She might have reread the first stanza of her draft and said, 'Wait—it needs something to wrap it up, to make it seem like it has ended. Then she probably read what she'd written out loud in different ways just to try it out one way and another way. Maybe after *bought me some soda and candy / ain't got it no more* she tried adding, *I'm sad about that*. Then maybe she reread what she'd written, crossed it out, and tried another ending."

"So for me, reading my poem and trying to make that poem sound right are big parts of writing poetry."

Link

Remind the children of the repertoire of things they might do today.

"Today during writing time, you have lots of things you can do. You can look again at your special objects and really look with poets' eyes, or you can work on turning your notes into poems. You can explore different ways to lay your poems out on the page. But I'd also like each of you to take at least a bit of time at the start of writing workshop to read your poems aloud over and over and decide how you want those poems to be read. Then change your words so they sound right."

Active Engagement

Ask the children to reread their poems and let rereading lead to rewriting.

"Let's get started on this while you're here on the rug. I'm going to ask partners to meet. Partner one, choose just one poem that you love and want to work more on. Read that poem aloud to partner two, and then the two of you will need to talk about what your words are saying and about how you can make your voice match the poem's meaning. Partner one can put notes beside your poem like I did when I wrote *Slow* or *Picture* it on 'Things.' As you do this, I bet you'll get ideas for changing the words—like we saw that Eloise Greenfield probably did while writing 'Things.' Just work with one of partner one's poems for now. I'll tell you when to switch. As soon as I see that you are working well, I'll send you off to partner one's writing spot to continue this work."

I'm not drawing on any special inside knowledge of Eloise Greenfield's revision process, which is why I preface all this by saying, "Eloise might have" or "Eloise probably." Whenever I want to show a product and teach children to emulate the process that led to the product, I have only a few options. I can rely on my own writing or on a child's writing, in which case I know the process as well as the product. Or I can re-create a published author's process either by relying on research about the author or by doing as I've done here and imagining the process an author probably used, making teaching points about that imagined process.

Notice that this link, like so many of them, reminds children of their growing repertoire of strategies. Because it doesn't take children long to do a bit of rereading, it's also possible to ask every child to spend a little time doing what I've taught them today.

This minilesson doesn't proceed in the usual sequence. It wasn't always thus. When we first wrote it, the active involvement came in its normal slot, but then we questioned why we wanted children to squeeze the rereading work (which was really the most important work of the day) into a three-minute slot within the minilesson.

We could have kept the active involvement in its regular position and, instead of having it be a time for children to reread their poems, they could simply have told their partner ways Eloise Greenfield made her poem sound good.

MID-WORKSHOP TEACHING POINT

Ask the students to listen to the songs in a few poems, to make sure they sound like music.

"Writers, may I stop you? We've been working today and yesterday to be sure our poems are like music, to be sure they have song to them and that their song matches their meaning. Let's listen to the song of a few poems before we write anything more. I'll read a stanza from each poem twice, and then I'm hoping you'll read the stanza aloud with me once."

"They sound different, don't they? Listen again. The music in poems can sound a lot of different ways."

I deliberately choose poems (or stanzas of poems) that are short because I can make my point more easily by quickly juxtaposing one poem (with its "songs") with another. The two poems have very, very different sounds, and each is very distinct. This is really the message I'm hoping to convey. I could have asked children to talk about the sound of each poem and the way it supports the poem's meaning.

Rope Rhyme
by Eloise Greenfield

Get set, ready now, jump right in
Bounce and kick and giggle and spin
Listen to the rope when it hits the ground
Listen to that clappedy-slappedy sound

Poem
by Langston Hughes

I loved my friend.
He went away from me.
There's nothing more to say.
The poem ends,
Soft as it began—
I loved my friend.

TIME TO CONFER

After introducing the abstract concept of music in spoken or written language, you can expect your children to approximate what they hear in published poems in different ways. Some children may copy, verbatim, one of the poems you have read together as a class. Approximating qualities of good writing by imitating the work of published mentors is a valuable way to develop one's own voice, and we need to congratulate our students for doing so. We need also to understand that young children want to be successful, and how better to achieve success than by writing a poem they already know is great? This being said, there are ways we can guide them toward their own voices.

You may want to have a content conference in which you encourage the child to go back to his own store of precious topics. With your support, he can find a way to honor a favorite poet while expressing his own thoughts. I often find myself saying things like, "I love Eloise Greenfield, too! She's great, isn't she? You know, we have this whole book of her poems, but what I'm really dying to hear is *your* words. Let's see if we can do what Eloise does, but using your ideas."

These conferences in *The Conferring Handbook* may be especially helpful today:

▶ *"Can You Think of One Moment That Holds the Big Feeling the Ocean Gives You?"*
▶ *"Are Those the Sounds You Hear?"*
▶ *"Can You Help Me See What You Saw?"*

Also, if you have *Conferring with Primary Writers*, you may want to refer to the conferences in part seven.

Celebrate the way one child used repetition to make her poem sound good. Read her poem.

"Writers, I've been noticing that you are doing lots of brilliant work to make your poems *sound* wonderful. Maddie tried a technique that Eloise Greenfield also uses. She found a key phrase and repeated it. [*Fig. III-2*] Remember how in 'Things' Eloise repeated *Ain't got it no more* many times? Well, listen to how Maddie, like Eloise, uses repetition to make her poem sound good."

Ask the children to show their partners any repetition or other strategy they've used. Listen in to what children are sharing and broadcast what you overhear.

"Would you get with your partner and see if you have used this same technique or whether you have used any other technique to make *your* poems sound good?"

Partners pulled close over each other's writing. Soon I called the class back together.

"Kids, I want to show you some other amazing things you all have done."

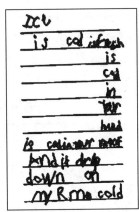

Ice
is cold, is fresh
is cold
in your hand
is cold
in your mouth
And it drips
down on
my arm
Cold

Fig. III-2   Maddie

When poets look at their work to see whether they've done a particular thing (as in this instance), you are making rubrics and criteria come alive. You may want to turn a share session such as this into a rubric. That is, each child could have a sheet that says "Ways to Make Poems Sound Good" and the class can compile a few goals, with each child copying them onto the sheet. Then each child can take any text he or she has written and check off if it does or does not exemplify each goal.

Bear in mind that many of the future sessions will help children gain more control over the sounds of their poetry. Rather than spending several days repeating this lesson, it may be more helpful to continue with the next sessions, each day reminding children to read their work out loud as they write. If you want to highlight the importance of reading drafts out loud, you could institute a new structure or tool that promotes rereading. For example:

- Pause each day's workshop five minutes before the end of writing time. Ask children to reread whatever they have written and to jot notes to themselves about what they plan to do next.

- When giving mid-workshop advice, ask children to stop writing, reread their work aloud to themselves, and then make decisions about the sound of it before continuing to write.

- If your children have older buddy readers, have your youngsters try to write in such a way that they signal to their older buddy how their poems should be read. The buddy can then read the younger child's poems out loud.

- Suggest to children that poems can sound different when they are read aloud in different spaces. If you have a parent volunteer who can help you, that parent might take a group of children on a poetry walk so they can read their poetry drafts aloud in the stairwell, the auditorium, the art-supply closet. . . . The point of this is not to perform the poems for others but to hear your own poems with attentive ears, realizing ways in which you could make it sound ever better.

There will be many times when the best way to assess your youngsters will be to take their work home and study what they've done on the page. For now, however, you'll do your assessing in the classroom. Much of the work you hope your children are doing is oral. You want them to reread, to listen to the words they have written, to try out their drafts by saying them aloud. This means that you'll probably want to stake out some assessment time while the students are writing. It helps to rope off some time in a public way. Ask children not to bother you, and tell them (and yourself) that when you see an issue, you can't and won't try to fix it. Instead, your goal will be simply to *understand* what your children *are* doing. That is, during the interval that you set aside for research—and it may be just five minutes—study the whole class with an eye only toward understanding, *not toward* rescuing, fixing, or redirecting. You'll probably want to stand back a bit during some of this research, literally counting up how many children are productively working, how many are rereading, how many are trying out different ways to write a single poem. You'll also want to pull in close and interview children to learn what they believe they were trying to do.

Expect to see trouble. If you don't see it, you are probably deluding yourself. Maybe some children reread by skimming, not lingering over and tasting and attending to their words. Maybe some children use the fact that you've asked them to reread their work often as an excuse to get very little written. Maybe some are writing poems that look like prose. In a story, the plot goes "One day, someone set out to do something. And then, there was trouble!" In a story, the presence of trouble is where the plot picks up its pace. The same is true in a classroom. Signs of trouble provide you with much of your curriculum . . . so look for it, prioritize it, and invent teaching which is responsive.

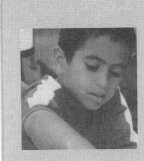

PUTTING POWERFUL THOUGHTS IN TINY PACKAGES

GETTING READY

- Tiny-topics notepads, recycled from your author study, for the end-of-the-day minilesson (you may need to make new ones)
- Chart titled "Strategies Poets Use"
- "Valentine for Ernest Mann" by Naomi Nye
- See CD-ROM for resources

THIS LESSON CREATES A BEND IN THE ROAD. *Until now, your children have been writing poems about a handful of small objects—little treasures—that you have set up around the classroom. Topic choice hasn't been a big concern, and children haven't been writing out of their own lives. Instead, the focus has been on writing with the form and language of poetry.*

But poets, even more than most writers, write from the heart, and they write about topics that matter. Today, you take your writers squarely back to the importance of topic choice and of writing about subjects that matter to them very much. You'll try to do this in ways that maintain the importance of writing with small, observant, honest details. Your goal will be to help your children write about big topics that matter while still writing with tiny details: a tricky balance.

THE MINILESSON

Connection

Recall and celebrate what your children have been doing as poets. Tell them poets also choose their own topics.

"In many ways, you've been writing just like real poets. You've tried to see with fresh eyes, to make your line breaks match your meaning, to listen for the song in your writing, and to write with honest words. But poets do one more thing." Stephanie paused to be sure all eyes were on her. "They choose their own topics and write out of their lives."

"We've been writing about little objects Lucy and I collected and laid out. Poets *do* often write about shells and pine cones and so forth, but in real life, poets aren't told, 'Here's a pine cone. Go write a poem about it.' Instead a poet—like every other kind of writer—needs to start by thinking, 'What matters to me?'"

"Today I'm going to teach you how poets choose topics and get started writing."

Teach

Tell the children that to get a good topic, you find a topic that feels big—and small.

"To get a good poem, I need a topic that is big—at least it needs to feel big to me, a topic that fills my heart—and I need a topic that is also small, like a safety pin, or like a one-moment story."

Planning curriculum, like writing itself, is challenging because the medium of time, like the medium of print, is linear and limited. We can't squeeze all we want to say into a single line that moves across the page—or into a single minilesson. We must make choices, lining up nonlinear concepts into a constrained sequence.

Writing a poem requires us to draw on six (or sixty!) concepts at once. A poem must have language, rhythm, form, line breaks, music, and meaning—all at once. But we can't convey this to children all at once. We could have simply told children to choose their topics without giving them instruction on this, but we worried that if given no instruction, children would go toward what they felt were poetic topics (spring, flowers, love).

In this unit, we decided to virtually assign children their content up front. Our focus all year had been content, and we wanted this unit on poetry to spotlight language. In any case, today we bring topic choice back.

The suggestion that poets write about something big that is also small is hugely significant and pertains to most (or all) writing, not just to poetry.

Demonstrate how you find a topic in your life that is both big—and small.

"I can start with something small, like the pine cone, and find out why it gives me a big feeling. Or I can start with something big, like how I love my niece Katie. That's a big topic, a watermelon topic; it gives me a big feeling."

"Remember when we studied Angela Johnson, we saw how she had the big watermelon topic of her son Joshua, but before she could write, she zoomed in on one moment when he heard night whispers? I'm going to do the same with my niece Katie because to write a poem, I need a big feeling, and I also need a topic that's small, like the acorns you've been studying or the leaf, like one safety pin or one moment."

"I could write a zillion poems and stories about Katie, but I need to zoom in on one small thing, and then I need to see that small thing with a poet's eyes, like you've been doing. So watch what I do."

"Let me see. Um, last weekend we went to the zoo together! That's still big. Um, I bought some food from the little machine so Katie could feed the sheep. At first she was scared to hold her hand toward the sheep's mouth, but then she did it."

"If I close my eyes, I can play that moment like a movie in my mind. Katie held her hand out like this." Stephanie reenacted how Katie gingerly held her cupped hand toward the sheep. "I can remember how it went." She paused and said, speaking now to the children, "Now I'm ready to write a poem because I have a big topic, a big feeling, and I have something small and detailed. I remember how we fed the sheep together."

Show the children a chart on which you've listed the steps you took.

"Did you see how I did these things?" Stephanie revealed this chart:

> ## STRATEGIES POETS USE
> ....
> * Poets find a big topic that gives them big, strong feelings.
> * Poets find a small object or moment or detail that holds the big feeling.
> * Poets look with poets' eyes and see this ordinary thing in a way.
> * Poets write about it, experimenting with line breaks.

If a writer starts with something small, it's helpful for that writer to reach for something big in which to couch that small detail. If a writer starts with something big (like "loving my mom"), it's wise for the writer to reach next for something small. This, again is a lesson that pertains to most writing.

Notice the cumulativeness of this teaching! Stephanie is harkening back to the author study work and its emphasis on writing not just about watermelon topics but also about seeds. She is referring to the children's work with Small Moments too. And she refers to children's efforts to see leaves and shells with poets' eyes.

Stephanie doesn't summarize her writing process, saying, "I considered lots of topics and then I selected one. I made a movie in my mind and then decided I was ready to start writing." Instead she reenacts the steps she went through so that kids empathize with her, living in her shoes and experiencing the process as she experiences it.

Active Engagement

Help the children coauthor the start of a poem about a shared big feeling.

"Let's try to get started on writing a poem together. Because we're doing this together, we need to think of a big feeling we all have, together. So, um, let's take this as our big feeling: loving to listen to a book. Get that big feeling, about loving listening to a story, in you right now." Stephanie paused to give them time to rev up their recollections of how much they adored listening to stories.

"Now would you look around the room and find something small that can hold that feeling for you. It can be an object, something you see—or it can be the memory of one particular moment. Tell your partner what the small thing is that holds the big feeling of loving to listen to stories."

"If you've got something small that holds this big feeling, will you signal to me? But don't do a thumbs up. Cup your hand like this if you've found a tiny object or moment that holds a poem, and I'll signal for you to tell us."

"I've got one," Samantha said, holding her hand out as if to show she held the pearl of an idea. Presenting what she hoped was the start of a poem, she said: "I love to read."

"What exactly do you see or do you remember that goes with that big feeling?" Stephanie asked.

Samantha pointed, "That's my place during read-aloud."

"That's smart, Samantha. You could get a poem out of that. Let's see. Um, could it start,"

> I have a place on the rug
> Where I sit during the read-aloud . . . ?

Samantha nodded.

Help children see the concrete detail with fresh eyes.

"Maybe you could think about what happens when you sit there, Samantha, and try to see that moment with fresh eyes, like you've been seeing your purplish stone with fresh eyes."

"I sit there and, um . . ." Samantha hesitated.

Stephanie doesn't give children a choice over the big topic, following the general rule that we engage children actively in the part of the process we are trying to spotlight at this moment, and expedite the other sections of the process by doing them ourselves.

Telling children that poets choose a big feeling or topic and then locate that big feeling or topic in something small feels impossibly complex. But when you scaffold children as Stephanie does here, the process is not so difficult.

Remember that many children benefit if you translate your big concepts into concrete, physical motions and objects, as Stephanie does here. She is picking up on something her children learned in earlier units which is an especially wise thing to do.

We call this "writing in the air." Stephanie is trying out one possible draft, dictating the exact words. When we want to show young children possibilities, instead of trying to explain a suggestion, we sometimes "write in the air."

Lucas, who was still holding his hand gingerly as if it contained the wing of a butterfly, piped up. "Samantha, maybe you can say you open the book 'cause you open it and the story comes out."

"That's beautiful. You are writing a poem already. 'I open the book. I see . . .' what? Lucas?"

Lucas thought, then recited, "'I open the book. I see dragons and stuff. You open the book, there is the story.'"

"Can you be exact? What story is it?"

"*My Father's Dragon.*"

"And soon, you are where?"

"Flying on the back of a dragon."

> I have
> a place
> on the rug
> where I sit
> during read-aloud.
> I sit there
> and my teacher opens *My Father's Dragon*
> and I'm flying on the back of a dragon.

Say the children's own words back to the class as a poem.

"What a poem! Listen," Stephanie said, and recited Lucas' poem.

Extrapolate the lesson you hope writers learn that pertains to another day and another text.

"Writers, do you see how Lucas and Samantha began with a general feeling of loving to read. Then they zoomed in on the moment when they sit in their reading spots, the book opens, and suddenly they are riding the backs of dragons! What a poem!"

Link

Remind children of what they learned today and how they might use it in their own work.

"So writers, when you finish writing poems about the stones and feathers, try finding topics in your own lives. For the rest of your life, when you want to write a poem, you'll go to something that is big—and is small, too. Get started on that now."

This is an example of the teaching method guided practice. Lucas is actively doing something—generating a poem— and Stephanie is using lean prompts to carry Lucas along through a process. In this way, Stephanie acts almost as training wheels, allowing Lucas to do something with her support which he couldn't yet do alone.

Later Stephanie will revisit this work and extrapolate lessons she hopes Lucas learns from the experience.

Stephanie's scaffolding has made a world of difference. Lucas couldn't have written this without her help. That's okay if Lucas and his classmates learn from this in ways that allow them to write more effectively another day, on another poem.

Use your hands to help children grasp the concept of zooming in on something small. Some children won't have a lot of frames of reference for understanding 'zooming in.'

TIME TO CONFER

This minilesson was challenging and important enough that you'll probably use your conferences to reiterate the minilesson. Plan to hold five or six conferences and then a strategy lesson. Tomorrow you can bring the stories of what individuals did today into a minilesson that reiterates this goal.

Children who are continuing to work on preexisting poems should be fine on their own. Look for children who are starting new poems. Their first job will be to get a topic that feels big to them—a topic that fills their hearts. If a child is having trouble finding such a topic, it's only because he is rejecting options too soon. You can say, "Just take one thing you love, I'll show you what comes next," making it easy for the child to write "Mom" or "Skateboarding" on top of the page.

Finding the one small object or moment that best holds the big feeling may not be as easy—but try encouraging the writer to brainstorm lots of possibilities: "Let me show you a strategy writers use a lot when we have a big topic and want to zoom in on a tiny detail that holds that topic. What I do is. . . ." Soon the writer will be listing small items under the umbrella topic.

Once the writer has selected one small object, moment, or detail, you'll want to focus on the subject. "I'm glad you chose that one! Tell me about it. Help me picture it." Be responsive to whatever the writer says.

These conferences in *The Conferring Handbook* may be especially helpful today:

▶ *"Can You Think of One Moment That Holds the Big Feeling the Ocean Gives You?"*
▶ *"Are Those the Sounds You Hear?"*
▶ *"Can You Help Me See What You Saw?"*

Also, if you have *Conferring with Primary Writers*, you may want to refer to the conferences in part seven.

AFTER-THE-WORKSHOP SHARE

Celebrate one child who found a big feeling and a tiny object or moment or detail that holds that feeling.

"I noticed a lot of great writing today! I'm so excited about what I'm seeing! I want to share with you a poem Hana wrote today. [*Fig. IV-1*] She really found a big feeling and a tiny moment that held that feeling. Let me read it to you."

"Can't you just tell how much Hana loves her cat? But she doesn't just come right out and say so. She finds a specific thing the cat does that really holds her love. Do you have any questions or compliments for the writer?"

Khalea said, "I like how you said the cat was licking your face instead of saying, 'I love my cat.'"

Daniel said, "I like how you put all the last three words on different lines, so we have to say, 'Licking / Your / Face.'"

Stephanie jumped in. "Wow! You are right, Daniel. I hadn't noticed that. Her poem almost goes lick, lick, lick, doesn't it?"

SECOND MINILESSON

Connection

Remind children that they are poets throughout the day, and recruit them to live in ways that let them find poems. Share Naomi Nye's poem "Valentine for Earnest Mann."

"Poets, before you go home, I want to remind you that we aren't poets for just one hour during the writing workshop. We are poets all day long. Today you will be walking home as a poet, entering your apartment as a poet, talking with someone at home as a poet, and going to sleep as a poet."

Kittens
A feeling
In the morning
A cat is
Licking
Your
Face

Fig. IV-1   Hana

If your children's feedback for the writer is more apt to be, "I like it" or even "I can picture it," don't decide your class is fundamentally different from this one! Children only respond with detailed feedback if you teach this. If your children aren't giving detailed, specific feedback, say, "I'm going to read this poem. I will want you to say in exact words the very particular thing you like about the poem. So listen up." Or even, "Tell your partner what you liked. Help each other say your compliment with a lot of detail." Or give them a copy and ask them to underline what they especially like.

Notice the importance of these graphic details. Details are important in minilessons, just as they are in students' writing.

"To write poems during our workshop time, you need to follow the advice of Naomi Nye. Remember earlier this year, we read her poem 'Valentine for Ernest Mann'? Remember how a child asked her, 'How do you make a poem?' and she answered:"

"Today and every day from now on, let's live in a way that lets us find poems."

Teach

Remind children of the tiny-topics notepads they kept earlier in the year, and suggest they revive these as places to record seeds of poems.

"Remember that earlier this year when we were learning to write like Angela Johnson, we kept tiny-topics notepads. If we were at home or at recess and we saw something tiny, something important that we knew we'd want to remember, we jotted it into our tiny-topics notepads. I think we need to begin to do that again, only this time you'll observe little tiny details (like shadows that drift across your ceiling) that could become seeds for poems. Write those down, and tomorrow in school we'll look at them like we've been looking at our shells and feathers."

Link

Give the kids notepads and remind them to pay attention to the poems hiding in their lives.

"So I'm giving you your tiny-topics notepads—and tonight, remember to follow Naomi Nye's advice and live in a way that let's you find poems. Pay attention. Notice the shadows drifting across the ceiling just before you wake up—and all the other poems hiding in your life. Bring your tiny-topics notepads to writing workshop with you tomorrow."

This is only the first half of Naomi's beautiful poem. The next image in it may be confusing for young children, but you can bring in the last few lines as well if you think it's appropriate.

Valentine for Ernest Mann
by Naomi Nye

You can't order a poem like you order a taco, walk up to the counter, say, "I'll take two," and expect it to be handed back to you on a shiny plate.

Still, I like your spirit.
Anyone who says, "Here's my address, write me a poem," deserves something in reply.
So I'll tell you a secret instead:
poems hide. In the bottoms of our shoes, they are sleeping. They are the shadows
drifting across the ceiling the moment before we wake up. What we have to do is live in a way that lets us find them.

Our curriculum should feel cumulative. Today's minilesson fits with and extends others that have gone before it in countless ways. The tiny-topics notepads are a perfect tool for this unit of study and deserve to be revived. They weren't given the spotlight they merit earlier.

We're bypassing the active involvement. It's time to go home!

FINDING INGREDIENTS FOR A POEM

GETTING READY

- Tiny-topics notepads with entries
- "Strategies Poets Use" chart
- See CD-ROM for resources

THE PREVIOUS SESSION ENDED with children being given tiny-topics notepads and encouraged to follow Naomi Nye's wise advice and live in ways that let them find poems, so they will arrive in school with written-down snippets of their lives. This minilesson helps children find one or two of these details that deserve to be made into poems. The real purpose, however, is to have a chance to restate that poems come from strong feelings and concrete details and to help children get the idea that topics for a poem are big—and small.

Even as I say this, I know it's not always true. Poets may simply revel in a sensory detail and enjoy finding the words and the form to capture that detail on the page. In a single unit of study on poetry, I can't show children the full breadth of the genre. It keeps me humble and tentative with children's work if I remember that much of what Stephanie and I teach contains important grains of truth but that our message isn't totally true. When we simplify concepts in order to teach them in strong, decisive ways, we reduce the true complexity and variety of a topic. That's okay . . . but it is important to stay humble.

Today, we'll help children choose from the topics they've gathered by reminding them that poems come from strong feelings and concrete details.

THE MINILESSON

Connection

Admire the way the children jotted down notes that promise to become poems—and tell them you'll teach them to select topics that could easily become poems.

"I had such fun greeting you all this morning because you all came in carrying ideas for poems in your tiny-topics notepads. David had seen the world like a poet and written about his trip to space right in his desk chair at home, and Abe had written about the pussy willows on his grandma's kitchen table. And many of you said to me, 'Is this a good idea for a poem?' That's a wise question because today and often in your life you'll need to sift through the observations and notes you gather and think, 'Okay, which of these could become a great poem?'"

Teach

Remind children that poems have ingredients. One ingredient is precise words. A second ingredient is music.

"Remember when we talked about how cakes have ingredients? As I told you before, poems have ingredients too. And lately we've been talking about a few of those ingredients. We said the first ingredient is that poets look at ordinary things in fresh new ways. The second ingredient is music. The music of poems comes from how the words are chosen and how they are put on paper.

"Writers, there is another ingredient I add to the mix if I'm trying to write a poem that I hope will be really special. I always try to have a big, strong feeling. So maybe I start a poem with a feeling of 'I love this classroom.' But then, I don't just put the feeling on the paper. I don't just say, 'The room feels special and I love it a lot.' Instead, I find something small that holds my feeling—and I write about that small object or that small detail or that small moment. I try to see that small bit of life in a fresh way *and* in a way that holds the feeling."

When I refer to the students' prior work, I don't generalize and say, "We've been studying poetry." That wouldn't be news to any of them! Instead, I try to recreate specifics of the previous lesson. Supplying examples of good student work provides students who are not yet on board with vivid and accessible illustrations of what I hope they will very soon do as writers. Finally, I tell them what I will teach them in this session.

This could also have been part of my connection. The components of a minilesson overlap.

This is a lot to tell kids, but mostly I am revisiting my earlier lesson. The new image of a recipe for poetry allows me to recall all I've taught before with a new twist.

I am demonstrating the exact same lesson that Stephanie taught yesterday when she gave Lucas guided practice in generating a poem about his love of reading that contained a big feeling and concrete details.

"Look again at yesterday's chart:"

STRATEGIES POETS USE
....

* Poets find a big topic that gives them big, strong feelings.
* Poets find a small object or moment or detail that holds the big feeling.
* Poets look with poets' eyes and see this ordinary thing in a new way.
* Poets write about it, experimenting with line breaks.

For any unit and for any writing workshop, a specialized language emerges, and this is lovely. Let yourself return to a few words often so your students internalize them.

Throughout this minilesson and the units there are phrases Stephanie and I use often:

▸ *Poets' eyes*
▸ *Topics that give a big feeling*
▸ *See the world like poets do*
▸ *Look at the world closely and carefully*
▸ *Small objects and details that hold big feelings*
▸ *Our poetry pencils*
▸ *The music of poetry*

Tell the children that when they reread their tiny-topics notepads looking for possible poems, they need to find topics they care about, that are very specific.

"So today and any day when you reread notes and ask, 'Which of these could make a good poem?' you need to ask, 'Do I have big, strong feelings about this?' Also ask, 'Have I found a moment or detail or object that holds those feelings for me?'"

Give a fictional example, one in which a child writes on a distant topic. Ask if that would have made a good poem.

"So let's say Robert had in his notepad, 'Franky has cool cars.' He'd need to ask, 'Do I have a strong feeling here?' I asked Robert, 'What is the feeling you get when you think about Franky's cars?' He shrugged and said, 'I don't know, really.'"

"So, poets, I think Robert could say, 'There's no poem here for me. This topic makes me go. . . .'" I acted out Robert's disengaged shrug.

One of the challenges in teaching young children is that your entryway into a concept needs to match theirs. Yesterday most of the children were just beginning to choose topics for poems, so I could address the dominant concepts in this lesson and the preceding one by discussing how to choose a topic and get started writing poems. But I know that these children will come to school with several possible ideas for poems in their tiny-topics notepads, so my approach, if it's going to align with theirs, needs to address the question of how poets reread, review, and choose between optional ideas for poems.

Suggest a second example, one that fits the criteria of being a good poem.

"Let's read the next thing Robert has written: 'My mother folds and pats the clean laundry like she loves my shirts.' I'm thinking Robert has got a huge feeling about his mother. But he doesn't just say, 'My mom is special. My mom is loving.' He finds a small moment—her folding and patting his clean shirts—that holds his feeling. He has definitely found the seed for a poem!"

Active Engagement

Ask the children to reread the notes they've written in their notepads, asking, "Does this have the ingredients to become a poem?"

"Now let's see if we can try what Robert did. Go ahead and open your tiny-topics notepads to the first empty page." I referred to the chart. "Look at what you wrote and ask, 'Does this give me a big, strong feeling?' Thumbs up if it does. Okay. Now ask, 'Have I found a small object or a small moment or detail that holds the feeling?' Tell your partner what you wrote and talk over if it is big and if it is small enough to make a poem."

Maddie said, "Well, I love insects, and I wrote about how a grasshopper's tummy is musical and its knees have ears."

Alex said, "I love recess, and I wrote about what I see when I look at the yard at recess, how all the kids are running around and playing."

Link

Encourage children to reread their notes, to think "What else is needed to make this into a poem?" and to draft poems.

"I know that today you'll reread the jotted notes you took yesterday in your tiny-topics notepads. Remember that," and here I essentially read from the chart, "we poets find a big topic that gives us big, strong feelings. We don't just put these feelings on the paper. Instead we find a tiny object or detail or moment—like feeding the sheep, or being woken up by the lick of a cat—that holds the big feeling. So if you are writing a poem that captures anger, you have to think of a moment or an object that holds your anger. If you are writing about worry, you have to have an object or a moment that holds your worry. If you are writing about your pride at baseball games, you need to zoom in on an

So far in this unit, you've probably given children six different examples of writers who use a concrete detail to convey a strong feeling. Children will learn more from examples than from instructions.

This activity gives vitality to any rubric or checklist and could be used regularly in your workshop.

In minilessons you'll only elicit input from a very few children. Be careful not to call just on those who you know will provide especially strong responses. It's important to bring out the full diversity of the class.

I deliberately choose big feelings other than love. I do this first because I noticed earlier when I eavesdropped on partnerships that most children—like Alex and Maddie— are writing about love. I also choose the feelings of anger and worry because I recall a writer who once said, "I don't write about my marriage much because I have a happy one." The writer went on to explain that he finds it hard to avoid clichés when writing about love and happiness. His words have stuck with me.

object or detail or moment that holds your pride. I can't wait to see the poems you write! Off you go!"

MID-WORKSHOP TEACHING POINT

If children form a line, wanting your help, intervene to remind them they can help each other.

"Writers, can I stop all of you? Would you *look* at what's following me?" I peered at the long line of children behind me. "Remember earlier this year when I told you that there's not just one writing teacher in this room, there are twenty-eight of you? Well, there's not just one (or two) *poetry* teachers in this room either! You can each be a poetry teacher."

"If someone comes to you and says, 'I don't know how to get started writing a poem,' what might you (as good poetry teachers) say?" I touched the chart to give them a hint.

STRATEGIES POETS USE
....

* Poets find a big topic that gives them big, strong feelings.

* Poets find a small object or moment or detail that holds the big feeling.

* Poets look with poets' eyes and see this ordinary thing in a new way.

* Poets write about it, experimenting with line breaks.

Melanie offered, "I could say, 'What do you have a big feeling about?' or if it's Marko, I could say, 'You *could* write about soccer.'"

"Smart work, Melanie. You can take over my job! What if the poet doesn't say, 'I don't know how to start,' but instead says, 'I'm done'?"

"You can tell her to write a new one?" Alex said.

"Yes, or you could suggest the poet reread the poem and change the words to make the music right. You all know a lot of ways to help each other. So right now, will everyone who is in line to see me go get help from a different poetry teacher—not from Stephanie or from me. We'll just listen in on and admire the way you all help each other."

This is a classic lesson. You can use it as a minilesson or as a share, if you prefer. The particular, new spin here involves asking children to use the chart you and the class have made together as a source of possible teaching points. It's crucial to direct children's attention to these charts.

Don't try to be comprehensive. If you suggest one or two things, children can discern the gist of what you are trying to say.

TIME TO CONFER

In the previous unit of study on nonfiction writing, the class progressed along somewhat in sync with each other. If your minilesson stressed the importance of making a Table of Contents for one All-About book, that day most of your children would be doing that work. This meant your conferences tended to echo the minilesson.

This unit of study is very different because the condensed nature of poetry means that children can cycle through the process of drafting and revising poems in short order. So, on any one day, you'll help one child find a focused, concrete detail to carry big feeling in his poem, and you'll help another child reread her finished work, listening to the sound she created with her line breaks.

It will help you remember your options if you carry your conferring guide sheet with you. Use it to help you notice what a child has done on his or her own with independence and tell the child what you see. Use the guide sheet also to remind yourself of the teaching points you might want to make as you move among your poets.

These conferences in *The Conferring Handbook* may be especially helpful today:

▶ *"Can You Think of One Moment That Holds the Big Feeling the Ocean Gives You?"*

▶ *"Are Those the Sounds You Hear?"*

▶ *"Can You Help Me See What You Saw?"*

Also, if you have *Conferring with Primary Writers*, you may want to refer to the conferences in part seven.

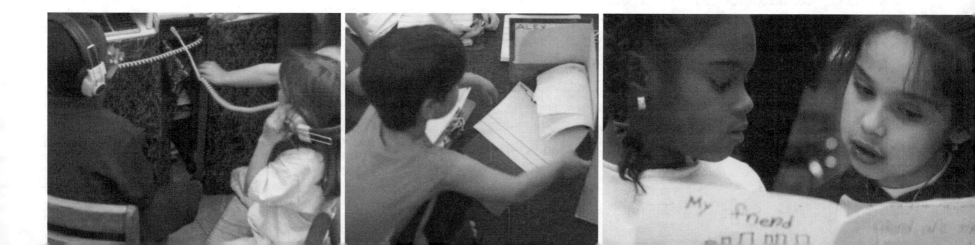

AFTER-THE-WORKSHOP SHARE

Remind the children that Naomi Nye believes that poems hide in the bottoms of shoes and that she calls us "to live in ways that let us find poems."

"Earlier today, we said that poems come from big feelings, but they live in the little details, the little moments. I think that is why Naomi Nye reminds us that poets live differently because we're always aware of the poems in our lives. Remember when she said, 'I'll tell you a secret,' and her secret was 'poems hide. In the bottoms of our shoes, they are sleeping. They are the shadows drifting across the ceiling the moment before we wake up. What we have to do is live in a way that lets us find them.'?"

Ask the children to find poems en route to the public library.

"We're going to be walking down the block to the public library soon, and I was thinking we should take our tiny-topics notepads and see whether we can walk to the library like poets and then be in the library like poets. If you find little moments or details or things that for you, for some reason, hold big feelings, jot a word or two in your tiny-topics notepad and tomorrow you'll have more time to write. Okay?"

This isn't a typical share session. Once you've established traditions, it's nice to deviate from them occasionally.

If you introduce (or reintroduce) a new tool, you have no choice but to keep it alive by incorporating it into your teaching for a few days.

▸ Revisit and tweak minilessons from earlier units of study in which you taught focus. Recall, for example, how you once asked children to make gestures to show whether a possible topic was a big, huge, armload-size watermelon idea or a tiny, tiny, handful-sized seed of the watermelon. The only really new thing you've said now is that, whereas authors of small-moment stories zoom in on a small moment, a poet writes about something that is both big *and* small—that is, *both* a watermelon-sized feeling and a seed-sized detail, object, or moment.

▸ Revisit poems you've read within this unit and ask, "What was the author's big, strong feeling (that he or she may not have come right out and named)? What was the tiny moment, object, or detail?" The truth is there are some poems that don't have both (Zoë's "Pencil Sharpener" may be an example) but these, and others, do:

Poet and Poem	Big Feeling	Details, Objects
Valerie Worth, "Safety Pin"	loving the poetic imagination	a safety pin looks like a small fish snapping its tail out on a thin shrimp with a surprised eye
Valerie Worth, "Aquarium"	marveling at the beauty of fish	flash gold and silver scales
Rebecca (student) "Things"	the beauty of fireworks and sadness when they are over	balls of fire burst forth the dark lonely sky
Eloise Greenfield "Things"	poetry is one of the best things to make	candy: ain't got it no more; sandcastles: ain't got it no more; poem: still got it

SHOWING, NOT TELLING

GETTING READY

▶ Poems written by the students in this class, in either this session or an earlier one

◉ See CD-ROM for resources

YEARS OF TEACHING MAKE IT EASY TO PREDICT *how students will react to our instruction. If we encourage descriptive words, we'll soon have a list of general, obvious adjectives in front of every noun: a cute puppy, a green dollar bill, a sandy beach. A lesson on writing with description will therefore need to be followed with one on selecting surprising descriptions: "the well-worn dollar bill," "the endless beach."*

Similarly, the previous lesson on the importance of selecting topics that hold big feelings will predictably lead youngsters to write with big-eyed sincerity about feeling "really, really sad" or "so, so happy." Follow-up minilessons will be necessary!

Earlier in the year, your children learned that writers have a saying "Show, don't tell." Instead of writing "I felt jealous of my brother's bike," a writer shows the feeling(s). "I looked at my brother's bike. . . ." Instead of saying, "My little brother was sad when he got sick in school and had to miss the field trip," it's better to show the feeling: "My brother sat alone on the bench at recess. He stared at the ground as if he didn't want to see the rest of his class waiting for their bus to arrive. I wanted to tell his class to stop bouncing around in excitement."

Today your lesson will be that poets, like writers of stories, know that one way to convey strong feelings is to show, not tell.

THE MINILESSON

Connection

Remind the children that poems have ingredients and usually these include big feelings and tiny details that hold the feelings.

"Earlier we learned that poems, like cakes, have ingredients. When someone goes to make a cake, they first put the ingredients (the stuff that will go into the cake) out on the table—the eggs, the cake mix, the oil."

"When we go to write a poem, we often start by being sure we have a big topic, one that gives us strong feelings. Then we think, 'Do I have a moment or an object or a detail that holds that big feeling?' But remember, I told you that poets don't usually just say their feelings straight out. Poets usually find moments or details that *hold their feelings*."

Tell the children that one way to convey feelings is through the strategy of "show, don't tell."

"Today, I want to teach you that one way poets do this is by showing, not telling."

Teaching

Remind your children of earlier work on "show, don't tell."

"Do you remember earlier this year when we wrote a story about how excited we were about our Thanksgiving party? Instead of *saying* we were excited, we *showed* it. We wrote: 'We kept popping out of the classroom door to see if anyone was coming yet. When Brandy saw our parents she called, "They're coming! They're coming!" and we all jumped up and down.'"

Tell the children that poets, like story writers, 'show, not tell' and that sometimes when we read a poem, we need to infer what the poet was trying to show us.

"It's not just story writers who show instead of telling. Poets do, too. This means that sometimes when we read poems we'll find that the poet comes right out and tells us the little details but leaves it up to us to figure out what he or

I've established the metaphor that poems are like cakes, made up of ingredients, and need to stay with this metaphor. If, on one day, I discuss the ingredients for a poem, I don't want to mix my metaphor by talking, the next day, about ways to nurture the seeds of poems! Either I am mixing, stirring, and cooking a poem or I am tending to it, weeding away the unnecessary bits, watching for signs of growth. A poem can't be cake-like and plant-like all in a day or two!

My lesson is on the importance of showing rather than telling, and so it only makes sense that I show rather than talk about the power of illustration.

If our point is that we're teaching writers strategies and goals they can use when they write, it's essential that earlier minilessons influence instruction several months later!

she is trying to show. The big feeling is usually there, but sometimes *the reader* has to say, 'Oh! I get it!'"

"I want to read you a poem that Sabrina wrote [*Fig. VI-1*] about a really cool thing she found at the beach. You'll see she doesn't say, "I found something really interesting and cool"—she *shows* it. Listen:

"If Sabrina had wanted to show that she despised this ferocious crab, she would have described the crab differently. Instead of saying *crawling* she might have said *writhing* or *grabbing* or *snapping*, and instead of *tickles* me she might have said, 'It pinches at me.' In the words we use, we *show* our feelings toward our subject."

Active Engagement

Read a few poems aloud and ask the children to name to their partners the big feeling and the small details.

"Listen to this poem about the underwater world Evan sees when he is snorkeling. [*Fig. VI-2*] Would you listen and then tell your partner what the big feeling is that Evan is trying to show, and then point to places where that feeling peeks through. First, I'll read and then you'll turn and talk with your partners."

Link

Encourage your children always to remember to find big topics that generate big feelings. Give some examples from your life.

"So, poets, I know that today and whenever we write poems, you will think about the big topics that fill you with strong feelings. For me, I'll think about feeling safe inside on rainy days or the pride at doing something new with my Frisbee. You'll think of your own big feelings. But remember that poets, like all writers, have a saying: 'Show, don't tell.' Instead of coming right out and telling us how you feel, you can show it by finding one time, one moment, and showing one bit of life."

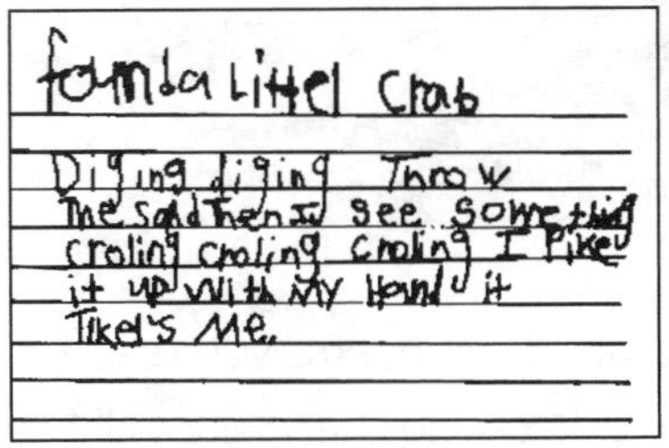

Found a Little Crab Digging, digging through the sand. Then I see something crawling, crawling, crawling. I pick it up with my hand it tickles me.

Fig. VI-1   Sabrina

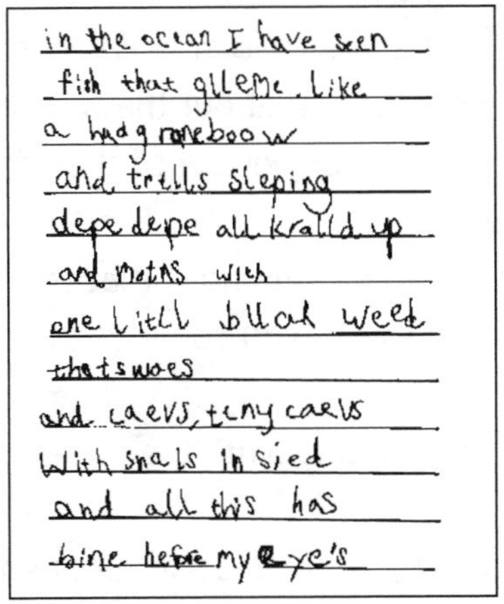

In the ocean I have seen fish that gleam like a huge rainbow and turtles sleeping deep deep all curled up and mountains with one little black weed that sways and caves, tiny caves, with snails inside and all this has been before my eyes.

Fig. VI-2   Evan

I include the detail about the Frisbee to be sure my examples will appeal to a wide range of kids. And I remind the children that poets, like all writers, know that one way to make a big feeling come to life is by "showing, not telling."

TIME TO CONFER

Your minilesson and some of the poems you read today, both, will have reminded children of small-moment writing. Recalling that work will be enormously helpful to children who, until now, may have been so worried about making their poems "poem-y" that they neglected to bring the true details of their lives to this new genre.

But you can be sure some children will feel stymied over the challenge to write poems (not Small Moment stories) about the tiny bits of their lives that matter enough to hold big feelings. Celebrate any evidence that children are struggling with this: this is a sign of awareness.

Name what you see. "So am I right that you're not sure how this will be a poem, not a story?" Then, when you come to the teaching component of a conference, you could:

▸ Teach children that many poets write their poems first as stories and only then revise them to make poems.

▸ Remind children that they know a lot about poems and can use what they know to write poems, not stories, about moments in their lives. They know about line breaks, for example, and about rereading what they write until the music is right. They also know about trying to see small objects with poets' eyes. The challenge will be to see small moments, too, with poets' eyes.

These conferences in *The Conferring Handbook* may be especially helpful today:

▸ *"Can You Think of One Moment That Holds the Big Feeling the Ocean Gives You?"*

▸ *"Are Those the Sounds You Hear?"*

▸ *"Can You Help Me See What You Saw?"*

Also, if you have *Conferring with Primary Writers,* you may want to refer to the conferences in part seven.

Celebrate the fact that the children have replaced vague words in their writing with more precise words. Give examples.

"Wow, this classroom is full of the amazing language of poets! All on your own you have invented ways to write with amazing language. You are taking your words (and especially action words) and making them exact. Today, when I came to Hana, I found she'd written, 'When my dog wakes up he goes to the kitchen!' but Hana had circled *goes* and tried other words, and now listen: 'When my dog wakes up he *gallops* to the kitchen!' I can just see that dog galloping across the floor! And when Ramon was writing about seeing a boy feed birds, he at first wrote that the boy gave food to the birds, but then he circled the word *gave* and tried it in a bunch more ways. Now he has, 'The boy *sprinkled* food for the birds.' Sprinkled! Amazing language!"

"Anna was writing a poem about eating ice cream in the summer [*Fig. VI-3*]. She could have said that when she eats an ice cream cone it *goes* down her hand, the ice cream doesn't just *go* down her hand, it *dribbles*. Listen."

"*Goes* wouldn't have shown the way the ice cream moves down her hand. So she sat there for a little while, really thinking about the exact right word for how the ice cream traveled down her hand. Finally, she chose the word *dribbles*, which is very specific."

"Writers, because we have so much amazing language happening in our room these days, what do you think about us having an Amazing Language Wall? We can put up bits of poems that are good examples of amazing language. I already put up one thing, from one of our favorite books. You know how Patricia MacLachlan describes the grass she loves in *What You Know First?* She doesn't just say that it was a lot of grass, she says, "an ocean of grass.""

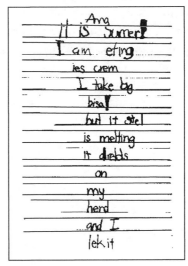

It is summer
I am eating ice cream
I take big bites
But it is still
Melting
It dribbles down
My hand
And I lick it

Fig. VI-3   Anna

Amazing language! I wrote it here on an index card and put it up on the wall. Hana and Ramon and Anna, during choice time, can you all write your amazing language on index cards and stick it up on our new Amazing Language Wall so we can all learn from you? And others, would you share your poems with your partner now? I'll give you an index card, and if you find amazing language in one of your poems, copy it onto this card and put it up."

Soon Daniel's entire poem [*Fig. VI-4*] had been posted on the bulletin board.

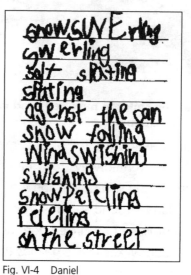

Snow swirling
Swirling
Salt spatting
Spatting
Against the car
Snow falling
Wind swishing
Swishing
Snow piling
Piling
On the street

Fig. VI-4   Daniel

- Throughout all of these units of study, we have taught many concepts by writing with the children about a shared experience. This method can work just as well for poetry. Gather the class in the meeting area and tell them that today they are going to help you write a poem about your walk to the park (or your visit to the aquarium or the day you and the children waited for the bus to show up or whatever). As you work together to create the poem, challenge the children (and yourself!) to use amazing language. The act of doing this together can yield wonderful results and can help young writers understand more clearly the concept of using amazing language.

- In her book *Awakening the Heart*, Georgia Heard describes an activity she calls "cracking open words," in which children use amazing language. Basically, children work to change isolated abstract sentences, such as "It was a nice day," into clear and specific sentences, such as "The sun was shining. A butterfly landed on my hand." In a minilesson, you could tell children that you found some bland bits in your poems and ask them to help you imagine more precise substitutes.

- Carefully chosen language is exact, honest, and often sensory. Ask children to use all their senses when they describe something—anything.

You'll find yourself sifting through reams of poems that your children write, looking for gems. Don't do all of this for them! You'll learn vastly more about your children's growing understanding of poetry if you ask *them* to reread everything and divide it into three piles. One pile could be for their most special poems, one for poems with something nice about them, and one for "not-the-best" poems. Then ask them to talk about what makes a particular poem from the best pile better than a poem from the worst pile.

When children use generic terms like "sounds nice" or "good words," ask them, "Can you show me where that is?" and "Explain what you mean." Of course, you'll have your own understanding of these terms, but if you want to understand your *children's* theories, *your* ideas are somewhat irrelevant.

When you conduct assessment interviews with children, keep in mind that your job isn't (at the moment) to *fix* what they understand. Your job is to honestly and clearly understand the ideas that are guiding your children. Later, you'll want to think, "How could what I see inform my teaching?"

HEARING THE VOICES OF POETRY

GETTING READY

▶ Three poems by students in the class, written in an earlier session, transcribed on chart paper (the poems should exemplify three distinct voices)

● See CD-ROM for resources

THROUGHOUT THIS UNIT, *you will run between one side of the ship and the other trying to maintain a balance, spotlighting first the content and then the form of poetry. You began with a session on seeing the world (one's topics) with a poet's eyes and then shifted to a series of sessions on line breaks and on revising poetry for sound. Then you ran to the other side of the ship to present lessons on choosing topics that generate big feelings and finding details that hold those feelings. Now you'll lead a session on the voices and points of view a poet can assume (the first of several sessions on the voices and language of poetry).*

Although you won't teach the terminology, you'll help youngsters consider the possibility of writing with lyrical, dramatic, narrative, or conversational voices. Your goal is to shake children free of mundane, ordinary language and help them invigorate their poems with poetic voice.

What do we notice poets doing?

-poets turn watermelon ideas into tiny seeds.

-poets use ~~boring words~~ poetic language

THE MINILESSON

Connection

Tell children that many of them are choosing great topics (ones with big feelings and small details) but that their writing then turns out to be "regular" and not poetic.

"We've been learning that although poets begin with strong feelings, they don't just pile those feelings all over the page: 'I *love* my cat. A LOT! She is cute and sweet.' or 'I *am so, so sad* because my flower died.' Many of you have tried to *show* that love or that sadness, those big feelings behind your poems. You are showing them with details, and sometimes this makes your poem feel very talky, and you come to me saying, 'This feels like regular writing, not like poetry.'"

Suggest the secret may lie in learning to take on the voices of poetry.

"Many of you are asking me, 'How do I make this into a poem?' and that's a big question. One way to turn regular writing into poetry is to give your writing the voice of poetry. Usually a poet doesn't take on an I'll-tell-you-all-about-this-thing voice." I said this in a blah, blah, blah way. "Today, I'll teach you the voices of poetry."

Teach

Help the children realize their poems may be talky. Do this by showing examples of the talky, ordinary language your children often use when they write.

"If you write like this—'Flowers. I love flowers. The tulips that I have beside my bed are yellow and blue' or 'Some flowers are alive, some flowers are dead' or 'Today my flower died and I'm sad because . . .'—your writing sounds regular."

This lesson will be urgently needed by at least half your class. You'll probably see your youngsters churning out poems, one similar to the next. This session can steer many of them away from that sort of writing. Be direct and to the point.

Pause for a moment to contrast the minilessons in this unit with those in the Launching unit. These are longer and more complex and ambitious. Your children should be ready for this sophistication by now, but if they aren't, simplify!

I select the topic of flowers because I'm about to juxtapose these talky versions of less-than-great poems with a poem that happens to be about flowers and is written in a poetic voice that is very easily identified, taught, and learned. When trying to show that one way of writing is preferable to another, it is important to keep as many things similar in the two versions as possible to highlight the one feature that changes. So in this instance, both the "bad" and the "better" poems are about dying flowers.

Suggest that one way to bring out poetic voice is for the poet to address the subject. Give an example that contrasts with the earlier ordinary versions you provided.

"One way to bring out the voice of poetry is to speak directly to the subject. Rebecca just did this in her poem [*Fig. VII-1*], which is about dying flowers but is written with poetic voice. She doesn't say, 'I want my flowers to open up. I know they will probably die soon.' Instead of writing *about* her flowers, she writes *to* her flowers."

Flowers, Flowers,
by my bed
Open up,
Like I said.
Lovely tulips
By my bed,
All three of you
Will soon be dead.
I will save both of you
I will water all six of you
And you will come back to life.

Fig. VII-1   Rebecca

Suggest that another way to bring out poetic voice is to tell a story with breathless urgency. Give an example.

"Some poems are story poems. The poet spins a story, like Ramon has done. [*Fig. VII-2*] To write a poem in this voice, imagine you've just run into the room and someone is there, and you breathlessly tell the story of what just happened."

"Listen to Ramon's story poem. Imagine he just ran into the room and he's telling you the story so you can picture what just happened."

"Did you hear that Ramon's poem tells the whole story, fast and urgently? Listen again, and picture that Ramon has just run in to tell us this really cool thing." I reread the poem.

Read the poem you select (as an example of a poet who writes in a storyteller voice) as if you've just run into the room; look at the children and try to tell the whole story with urgency. Spit it out.

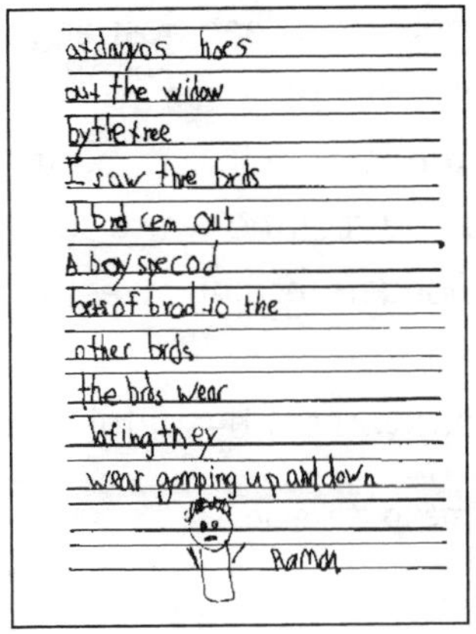

At Daniel's house
Out the window
By the tree
I saw three birds
One bird came out
A boy sprinkled bits of bread
To the other birds
The birds were laughing
They were jumping
Up and down.

Fig. VII-2   Ramon

Suggest yet a third way to write poems, in a lyrical fashion, but don't use the term! Give an example.

"Some poems sound like the poet is speaking right to you and saying something that is the deepest, truest sound of his heart or her heart. Listen to this poem that Susie wrote yesterday. [*Fig. VII-3*] Listen for how this poem is like the song of her heart."

Active Engagement

Invite your kids to try saying a poem in different voices. Give them a topic and a context. First, set things up so that they speak to the subject of the poem.

"So let's try it. Pretend you are writing about waking up in your bed this morning and finding it is sunny already. You *could* say," (my intonation suggested these would be blah options) "'Some mornings are sunny' or 'Today when I woke up, I saw some sun.'"

"But pretend you are in bed, just about to wake up, and you feel the warm sun. Partner one, tell partner two a waking-up poem you would say, speaking directly to the sun. Picture it, partner one. You are lying in bed, just starting to wake up. You feel the warm sun on you, and you say to the sun. . . . what?" The children began reciting sweet messages to the sun, and I listened to a few of them.

"Writers, I heard you say beautiful poems," I said. "Leo said,"

Sun, I know it's time to wake up.
I feel you there.
Let me lie here.

"That's one way to use the voice of poetry."

Read this poem with a full heart. The poet is bursting with solemn gladness, savoring each precious detail of her home. Practice it beforehand to get the rhythm right—I think it's written in couplets even though she hasn't spaced it that way.

My House
When I walk in the door
I have love for where I am
I can see everything
I want to see
I can do anything
I want to do
I go to my room
and there is my glory
It's what I want
To Be
It's Home.

Fig. VII-3   Susie

The easiest kind of active engagement would be to say, "Turn to your partner and say back three ways to turn regular-sounding words into poetry." That'd be a fine option, but it's always preferable to get children to do what you want them to do rather than talk about it.

I sequence my comments so the last thing I say sets up the children for just what I want them to do. This provides a lot of support.

One example is enough. You have lots of voices to illustrate.

Now ask the kids to use a storyteller voice to say aloud a poem about the same topic, written as if they were blurting out the whole story.

"Now let's try a different poetry voice. Partner two, tell the story of waking up to partner one using a storyteller poet voice. Pretend you just got to the breakfast table and you're about to blurt out the whole story of how the sun woke you up. Maybe start it like this: 'All night, I lay in bed, sleeping.' Turn and talk."

Now ask the kids to try on a lyrical voice.

"Now get a feeling in your heart about waking up and feeling the sun. Think about the deepest, truest thing you have to say about waking up and feeling sunshine. Partner one, start a poem: 'I wake up, I feel. . . .'"

Link

Remind writers that if their poems sound like regular writing, they can try writing in one of the voices of poetry.

"Writers, if you worry your poems sound too 'regular,' remember that you can try on the voices of poetry. You can write *to* your subject, you can use a storyteller voice, you can try to write straight from the heart. If one of you wants more help writing in the voices of poetry, stay behind on the carpet and I'll help you. The rest of you—off you go."

MID-WORKSHOP TEACHING POINT

Intervene to explain yet another voice poets can use, this time one a child has discovered. In this instance, it is using dialogue.

"Writers, Evan has found another poetic voice. He's realized that in a poem, two people can talk to each other. If you use their real, true voices, if their voices ring true, it can be a beautiful poem. Listen, in Evan's poem [*Fig. VII-4*], for the voice of David, who comes over and is really mean. Listen to hear David's voice."

You may be thinking, "There is no way my children can learn all these voices of poetry, especially not when they have all these options thrown at them so fast." You're right! This is an exposure minilesson, and the intention is to mention, to touch on, to suggest possibilities. Children won't learn the particular voices you discuss, but they can glean a general sense that poets write differently.

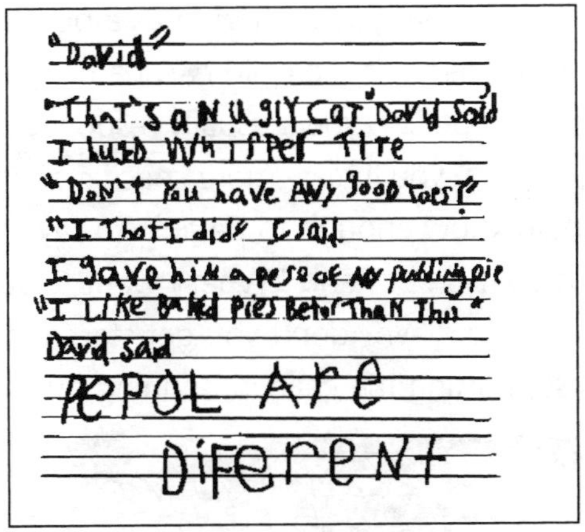

Fig. VII-4   Evan

"David"
"That's an ugly cat," David said.
I hugged Whisper tight.
"Don't you have any good toys?"
"I thought I did," I said.
I gave him a piece of my pudding pie.
"I like baked pies better than this," David said.
People are different.

TIME TO CONFER

You've given your youngsters lots of options and asked them to practice and experiment with those options. Now you need to let them make their own choices and carry out their own intentions. Expect your children to approach writing with deliberate plans and intentions. Begin your conferences by asking, "What are you working on today as a poet?" If the child answers vaguely, you can push for a more specific answer: Tell them, "Remember that in conferences, your job is to say what you are trying to do as a poet. You might, for example, say you're doing any one of these things on the chart [reread it] or you might say something else. But when I ask, 'What are you working on?' you need to tell me." If the child still can't articulate what he or she is working on, say, "Show me what you've done," and then interview the child to elicit more information. Finally say back to the child what you have heard ("So am I right that what you are doing as a poet is . . . ?").

On the other hand, if the child can name what he or she is working on (and most will be able to do so), you'll usually respond, "So can you show me that?" After you look at the work, you'll have more specific questions. Once you get answers to them, you should know enough to be able to say to the child, "What I'm noticing about you as a poet is . . ." and "What I want to suggest is. . . ." You may end the conference by saying, "Why don't you get started on that while I'm here," and then coaching and supporting the child in bringing out the details.

These conferences in *The Conferring Handbook* may be especially helpful today:

- ▶ *"Can You Think of One Moment That Holds the Big Feeling the Ocean Gives You?"*
- ▶ *"Are Those the Sounds You Hear?"*
- ▶ *"Can You Help Me See What You Saw?"*

Also, if you have *Conferring with Primary Writers*, you may want to refer to the conferences in part seven.

AFTER-THE-WORKSHOP SHARE

Tell your children their work has given you goose bumps. Set them up to read aloud to their partner in ways that give each other goose bumps.

"I have goose bumps over what you all have been writing today. Would you give your partner goose bumps?"

"Get together. Partner two goes first. Look over your poem first so you have it in your heart and you are ready. Then your job is to read your poem aloud in a way that gives your friend goose bumps. Read it once, then let there be silence. Then read it again. Afterward, your job, partner one, will be to tell partner two what his poem or her poem made you feel. Say *a lot of words* to go with the feeling that you have. Then you can switch roles."

"So remember, partner two: Read your poem to yourself first so you're ready. Then read your poem—just one poem that you choose—aloud to give your friend goose bumps. Read it twice. Then, partner one, talk about what you felt. Then switch roles."

You'll see that reading aloud plays a big part in this unit of study. I believe that children write 'up' if they plan to read their writing aloud beautifully.

Notice that the last thing I do before I send children off is reiterate the heart of what I want kids to do.

Remember that these are very young children. It is not the least bit important that they be able to recite back to you the different voices in which poets write. But it is very important that they understand that poets care about the sounds of their words. If your children haven't done choral or dramatic readings of poems in which they talk through how to read one line or another and whether to incorporate gestures, you may want to do so now. Use Eloise Greenfield's "Things" or David McCord's "This Is My Rock" or Lilian Moore's "Go Wind." Or try an excerpt from Christina Rossetti's "The Caterpillar."

Recruit the class to help a child who feels that her poems all sound too regular. "If she wanted to write this in a talking-to-the-subject voice, like Rebecca talked to the tulips by her bed, how could she? Tell your partner."

Tell the class about one child who got sort of confused about the options he had. "So Ramon suggested we make a chart and put examples of each kind of voice on it. Then he could go to the chart and read those examples and remember how the poem goes. Let's read some poems and decide which category that poem belongs to." (Every partner team can have a short stack of examples to file, too.)

Go Wind
by Lilian Moore

Go wind, blow
Push wind, swoosh.
Shake things
take things
make things
fly.

The Caterpillar
by Christina Rossetti

Brown and furry
Caterpillar in a hurry;
Take your walk
To the shady leaf or stalk.

SPEAKING TO THE OBJECT:

"Sea Shell"	Amy Lovell
"Tree at My Window"	Robert Frost

STORYTELLING VOICE:

"Paul Revere's Ride"	Henry Wadsworth Longfellow
"The Owl and the Pussycat"	Henry Lear
"Fun"	Eloise Greenfield

LYRICAL VOICE:

"Dust of Snow"	Robert Frost
"Honey, I Love"	Eloise Greenfield
"This Is My Rock"	David McCord
"Poem"	Langston Hughes

CONVERSATION:

"Mother to Son"	Langston Hughes
"Old Man Ocean"	Russell Hoban

SEARCHING FOR HONEST, PRECISE WORDS

GETTING READY

- One of your poems, written on chart paper—be ready to circle a vague word and to generate a few more precise substitutes
- Shared-reading pointer
- Blank chart paper and marker
- "Strategies Poets Use" chart
- See CD-ROM for resources

IN THE PREVIOUS SESSION, *you helped children who felt their poems were mundane and regular. Today, you'll extend that work. This time, instead of addressing the voice and point of view of a poem, you'll focus on the language. You'll encourage children to search for the precisely right word.*

In this yearlong curriculum, poetry will teach your children to learn to care about the language they use when they write. Other units of study have highlighted details, structure, and clarity in writing. This unit will spotlight words themselves. You will encourage children to love words, to listen to them, and to choose them with care.

You will not urge children to use "beautiful" or "descriptive" language but will instead advocate precise, honest words. You'll encourage children to reach for the word that exactly matches what they are trying to say.

The Minilesson

Connection

Celebrate that children explored poetic voices. Tell them you know some of them still feel that their poems are prose.

> "Yesterday you did a lot of wonderful exploration in order to make your poems *sound like* poems."

> "A few of you are still worried. 'How can I be sure I'm writing a poem, not a story?' It's true that some poems feel very close to stories—but always, when you write a poem, you want to take extra special care of one thing . . . your words."

Tell the students that today you'll teach them to reread for honesty and to revise words until they're precisely right.

> "Poets spend a long time searching for the exact word to match what they want to say."

> "Yesterday I wrote a poem about my mom and then I reread it and I asked, 'Am I saying exactly what I want to say?' This is the poem I wrote."

The preceding session was layered and complex. Today you return to a straightforward and more accessible point. Both these minilessons work together to help children care about their language.

It is so important that we teach children to reach for exact, specific, true words rather than for fancy words. You'll notice that neither Stephanie nor I ever exult the advantages of "beautiful words." Instead, we talk up "precise words."

My Mom

In my lunchbox
A frozen juice
Because it's hot today
wrapped in paper
So it won't melt
How come I never
Ever
See her
Do this?

"I went back to this word, *wrapped*. I realized it wasn't the exact, true word, so I circled it and then, over here, I listed other ways to write the true word. I wrote bundled, *held*, and *nestled*. Poets do that."

"Today, you'll all learn that when we poets reread our poems, we ask not only 'Does this sound right?' but also 'Is this the true thing I want to say?' Sometimes we find words (or sections of our poems) that aren't exactly true, so we try them again. I'll show you how to do that."

Teach

Tell a story about a person who searched for the exactly right words, tried generalities, and settled on a fresh metaphorical way to describe something.

"Listen to this story. Yesterday, my friend Emily called me on her cell phone from the beach and she said, 'I called because there is something so beautiful here and I need to tell you about it.' It turned out there were these shells all over the beach that seemed amazing to her. She said to me, 'They're little, and small, and nice, and purpley, and little.'"

"I said, 'Emily, I can't picture them! Help me picture them.' So she said, 'They're tiny purple mussel shells, open, but still connected, and they look like, like, like a million tiny purple butterflies flying in the sand.' When she said that, all of a sudden I could see it!"

"My friend Emily really searched for the exactly right words to tell me about the shells. That's what poets do. She was looking at the shells right in front of her, searching for the words that would really match what she saw. 'A million tiny purple butterflies, flying in the sand.' Today we're going to learn how to search for the exact words that match what we're seeing."

It's wise of Stephanie to tell the step-by-step story of how she went about revising her words rather than simply showing children that she revised. Her step-by-step story teaches kids a process they, too, can try.

When you write texts as examples, it's great to make them close to the sort of thing your children could write. The topic and simplicity of this poem make it a perfect one, and you could revisit it in future minilessons in which you teach the power of detail and of show-not-tell.

This is an ambitious connection; the latter portion could be the teaching component in a less packed minilesson.

This tiny anecdote is worth studying. What makes it so effective? I think it profits enormously from the image of Emily on the beach with her cell phone in hand; we can see the scene, and there is an urgency that comes with Emily trying to transmit the image of the beautiful shells into the very concrete and constrained cell phone.

Children use simile and metaphor naturally and without self-consciousness. "He had a jelly-bean bald head," a five-year-old said to me. "This blanket is my magic cape." "My pancake is swimming in an ocean of syrup." It's wise to nudge children to use figurative language, but let's stop filling their heads with worry about the differences between simile and metaphor. We can save all the formal definitions and differentiations until they're a bit older.

Active Engagement

Ask the children to work on a shared poem about some everyday object. In this instance, the class tries to collect accurate observations about the shared-reading pointer.

"Writers, today let's begin work on a poem while we sit here on the rug. I was thinking we could try writing a poem about this pointer; we use it every day and it helps us read. So let's first think about what we want to say about the pointer—tell your partner." The room broke into a buzz. "Poets, I heard Kylene tell how we hold the pointer. So let's all of us really watch how I'm holding the pointer. I'll hold it and do some work with it, and would you tell your partner *the exact true thing* you really see me doing with the pointer? That's what poets do. We try to find the exact true words, like Emily did when she saw those shells."

Again, we are very detailed ("Tell your partner the exactly true thing you really see me doing with the pointer") and then we back up and extrapolate the larger lesson ("that's what poets do. We try to find the exact true words.")

Collect ways to describe the pointer.

Soon the class has accumulated a list:

- Stephanie holds it like a stick.
- Stephanie points the pointer at the words.
- Stephanie holds it like a wand.
- When Stephanie points at a word, we say it and it's like the word comes to life.
- The pointer taps and the story pops out, piece by piece.
- It's like the guy at the concert who points to the drums.

This list is long enough. When literacy specialist Marie Clay toured our reading and writing workshops last year, she said, "Generally, once a list holds more than three or four items, it ceases to be useful." After a while, the reader of a list should be able to fill in the "and so on, and so on."

Tell the children that poets brainstorm possible ways to say something and select a way that is true.

"Often poets do this—they try lots of ways of describing what is true and then they reread and think, 'Which is honest and fresh and sounds right?' Would you and your partner reread all we've written about the pointer and find ones you like? Maybe put two together. Be sure what you say is true and that it sounds good!"

We repeat the goals over and over. One is honesty, one is sound. Writing poetry involves juggling these two concerns, keeping both in mind at all times.

Link

Remind your children that they now have a repertoire of strategies for writing poetry—and invite them to use any of these strategies.

"So, poets, we've begun to grow a whole list of strategies poets use to write poems, and today you can do *any of these things* or you can invent new strategies. Come get me if you invent something new so I can admire what you have done." Stephanie added an item to the chart the class had been making so it now looked like this:

STRATEGIES POETS USE

* Poets find a big topic that gives them big, strong feelings.

* Poets find a small object or moment or detail that holds the big feeling.

* Poets look with poets' eyes and see this ordinary thing in a new way.

* Poets write about their topic, experimenting with line breaks.

* Poets reach for honest, precise words.

Notice that whenever possible, our minilessons end with us adding the new strategy to children's ongoing repertoire.

Time to Confer

As you walk around the classroom conferring today, you will notice children who need support in several different ways. Keep in mind the chart "Strategies Poets Use," and be aware that each of those items can require a separate conference. Often first graders have a hard time telling us what they are working on as writers. This may be a good time to help children become better at naming what they need to work on as writers. You may find yourself giving students support using any of the following prompts:

- "Can you tell me what you need to work on most as a writer today?"
- "Do you think you might need to work on one of the strategies on our chart today?"
- "It seems like you could work on reaching for honest, precise words in this poem."
- "Reread your poem and tell me where you might want to do some work."
- "I'm noticing that when you write poems, you often do. . . . But I notice you've never tried. . . . Can I help you to try that strategy with this poem?"

These conferences in *The Conferring Handbook* may be especially helpful today:

- *"Can You Think of One Moment That Holds the Big Feeling the Ocean Gives You?"*
- *"Are Those the Sounds You Hear?"*
- *"Can You Help Me See What You Saw?"*

Also, if you have *Conferring with Primary Writers*, you may want to refer to the conferences in part seven.

School is like a fun place.
... walking into a cloud.
... heaven.
... a beautiful castle.
.. a flower blowing around the sky
.a place in the sun.
glitter flying around

Help the children practice finding honest, precise words with their partners to describe something in the room.

"Today we talked about how poets reach for honest, precise words. Let's try it together. Would you look at our fish tank and tell your partner what the goldfish looks like? Use precise, exact words!" Children talked to their partners.

"Now tell your partner how the fish moves."

Read to children another example of honest, precise language.

"Let's look again at Valerie Worth's poem and notice how *she* tried to say exactly what *she* saw. I'll read her poem. Will you notice the exact, precise words she uses and see if you can get hints from what she's done? After all, she's a professional poet and we're learners. So listen to what she wrote, and talk about how you could learn from her." Stephanie read the poem.

Help the children practice choosing the right words by using a line from a child's poem as an example.

"Now, Michael has been very brave and generous today and is going to let us help him with a line of poetry he's been working on."

Stephanie had written on a chart, "The volcano talks and spit comes out."

You'll recall that I often show children two versions of something—anything. If I want to show them a strong lead, I juxtapose it with a weaker one. If I want to teach "Show, don't tell," I first show children what it would be like if I just named a feeling. Here, you recruit children to produce the "Before" version, asking them to describe the fish. Then you juxtapose what you've done with what Valerie Worth did, writing on the same subject. "Let's see if we can pick up hints," you can suggest.

Goldfish
by Valerie Worth

Flash
Gold and silver scales;
They flick and slip away
Under green weed—
But round brown snails
Stick
To the glass
And stay

Notice the action words that Valerie Worth uses. Children often think that poetic writing means writing with lots of descriptors. When I studied writing, my teacher told me that adjectives and adverbs are usually signs of weak nouns or verbs. The young dog could be better described as a puppy. If the man walked lazily, it'd be better to say he ambled. If she talked quietly, couldn't one say she whispered?

"So far, Michael has 'The volcano talks and spit comes out,' which is really starting to give me a picture in my mind of what a volcano might do. I'm looking at these two words, though." Stephanie used a marker to make boxes around the words *talks* and *comes*. "And I think we might be able to find a more specific way to create an image. We could replace *talks* and *comes* with really strong words."

"Okay, so writers on my right, work with partners to think of more specific words to put in the place of *talks* and partners on my left, do the same thing for *comes*. Show me a thumb when you think you've got something really specific."

Aidan said, "I think you could put *screams* where *talks* is."

Gaby offered, "And I think you could put *shoots* where *comes* is."

Stephanie became really excited. "Wow, let's read it that way and see how it sounds. 'The volcano screams and spit shoots out.' Whoa! That's a whole different volcano from the one we had before, right?" Stephanie wrote these two new words under the words they could replace on the chart. "Let's hear a few more for *talks*."

Sarah said, "*Hollers*."

Daniel suggested, "Or you could say *sighs*. That's really different!"

Stephanie moved the class along. "And how about a few for *comes*?"

Anna said, "*Dribbles*! Like my ice cream!"

Klara contributed, "*Flies*."

Rob came up with, "*Sprays*."

Remind children to choose honest, precise words in their own writing.

"Well we have definitely learned something about choosing words, right? A volcano can dribble and that is completely different than a volcano that sprays. Let's really make a commitment to find the best, most specific words for our poems from now on."

You may want to teach children that poets often choose words that sound and feel like they mean. The word hop *almost hops out of the mouth, and the word* sprawls *can't keep from sprawling. There are lots of other words for which sounds match the meaning: an* elephant *just has to be fat and big, and a* worm *has to squirm. The name* Jell-O *jiggles and wobbles, and pointy* pinpricks *make a sharp, stabbing sound.*

Notice that we ask children to turn and talk with their partners before we elicit these responses from particular individuals. This allows every child to be active and interactive. If you simply call on the children who raise their hands, only a handful of children do the mental work of producing their own response to your questions.

If Children Need More Time

- Ask children to look again at the words Valerie Worth and Rebecca have used in their poems. You might say something like, "When Valerie Worth says that the goldfish 'flick and slip away,' I think she must have really watched the goldfish, searching for the exact words to describe how they move. And when Rebecca said the fireworks are 'bursting into bloom,' I know that she was watching those fireworks, trying to get the exact words that would describe how she saw them. These poets both searched for the exact *right* word to describe what they saw. It was not important to find an exciting word or a long word; they searched for the right word, the word that matched what they saw." You could ask children to reread their poems and circle words that aren't yet the precisely right words. Later, during the writing workshop, they may try to find the more accurate word.

- If your point is simply to emphasize that poets choose words carefully, you could copy a poem that the children don't know onto chart paper and cover a few especially apt words with sticky notes (you may already do this during shared reading). Then tell children that the poet probably paused for a bit, thinking, "What word *might* I use right here?" and then maybe listed options and chose one. "What words do you think he listed as options?" you could ask, and in this way set up children to imagine and choose between possible ways to say something.

PATTERNING ON THE PAGE

GETTING READY

- Necklace made out of patterned beads
- Chart with Lilian Moore's "Go Wind" written on it
- Blank chart paper and marker
- Examples of poems with patterns
- See CD-ROM for resources

BEFORE LEAVING YOUR EXPLORATION into the sounds of poetry, you want to remind children that poetry is often patterned. Patterns play a big role in the math curriculum in many primary classrooms. Children should be accustomed to seeing patterns in objects and numbers, so it's not a gigantic step to remind them that patterns are also important in poems.

You will touch on the importance of repetition and of a list structure in poems, but your emphasis will be that poets use patterns to support their meaning.

THE MINILESSON

Connection

Show the children a necklace one child made out of patterned beads and ask children to notice the pattern. Tell them poets, too, like patterns.

"This morning, Sarah showed me a necklace she made. Sarah, stand up so everyone can see it. Isn't it beautiful? She made a pattern, didn't she! Can you see the pattern? Note in your mind how the pattern goes on Sarah's necklace." I paused.

"The reason I'm telling you about Sarah's necklace is that poets think a lot about patterns when they write. Today, I want to teach you the power of patterns in poetry."

Teach

Tell the children that patterns are important in the world. Remind them of patterns they know well.

"Patterns are really important in the world: in math, in building, and in art."

"Remember, when we look at the calendar, we see that weeks are *always* seven days long; they *always* have five weekdays (Monday, Tuesday, Wednesday, Thursday, Friday) and two weekend days (Saturday and Sunday). That's a pattern, an order."

And a day always begins with the sun coming up." I pointed to the horizon, where day breaks. "And then the sun moves until it's over our heads at noon, and then the sun goes down and it is night. That's a pattern, an order."

"And there are patterns in buildings—maybe a building has a door in the middle of a row of all the same windows on this side and a row of all the same windows on that side. That's a pattern, an order."

"And Sarah's necklace has five blue beads, then three silver dots, then five blue beads, then three silver dots. That's a pattern, an order."

One powerful method for teaching a concept is to reduce that concept to its simplest form, teach it in that form, and then show how it translates into more complex situations.

If you look across minilessons, you'll see that they—like conferences—employ four teaching methods (demonstration, guided practice, explicity telling then giving an example, and inquiry). I often describe the explicitly-telling-then-giving-an-example method as the teacher giving a small, memorable keynote address. It is the hardest method to use. This minilesson offers a good example of one where the method begins as explicitly telling and then showing an example.

"Patterns are about having an order, a plan, and keeping things in that order, that plan. Poems often have a pattern, an order. Sometimes the whole poem stays in the same pattern, the same design, and sometimes a part of the poem is patterned."

Ask the children to look now at a poem, not a necklace, and try to join you in discerning the patterns. Show them what you mean by finding one pattern, then ask them to find another.

"Let's look back at poems we've shared to see if we can find the pattern in the poems just like we tried to see the pattern in Sarah's necklace."

"Let's look again at Lilian Moore's 'Go Wind.' Remember that earlier we noticed she isn't writing *about* the wind, she is writing *to* the wind. Now, I want you to notice the patterns in her poem. There are a lot of them. Listen while I read it."

"So one pattern I'm noticing is that here—the first two lines—and here— at the start of the third stanza—she has almost the same pattern with little changes. She says, 'Go wind, blow / Push wind, swoosh,' and 'Go wind, blow / Push things—whew!' like that."

Notice that when I make my little speech about patterns, I do so in a way that employs patterns. It's often wise to make our form match our message.

This will work best if your children have already read and enjoyed this poem. It is rare for us to introduce a text for the very first time in a minilesson.

I find a pattern that is not totally obvious, leaving the more obvious ones for kids to find. In a moment I'll pass the baton to the kids and ask them to take a turn searching for patterns, and I want to set them up for success.

Go Wind
by Lilian Moore

Go wind, blow
Push wind, swoosh
Shake things
Take things
Make things
fly.

Ring things.
Swing things
Fling things
high.

Go wind, blow
Push things—whew.
No wind, no
Not me—
not me.

Active Engagement

Ask the children to find another pattern (or two) in the same poem.

"Let me read it again, and then you will tell your partner another pattern you notice."

I read it aloud, and they turned and talked, quickly identifying the list-like structure at the center of the poem.

Remind writers always to think, 'Should this poem have a pattern?' and to be sure the poem's pattern matches its meaning. Ask children to try creating a pattern for a very simple poem you give them.

"So, writers, I hope if you start a new poem, today or any day, you might think, 'Should this poem have a pattern? How should it go?'"

"Let's try thinking like that. Let's say you want to tell about how your baby brother keeps on interrupting you. You start to play or to talk, then he gets in the way. It keeps happening. Tell your partner how your poem could be patterned in a way that might make sense." Partners talk with each other. "I heard you say your poem might go, 'I play airplane. My brother interrupts. I build bridges. My brother interrupts. I make sand castles. My brother interrupts,' like that. Smart idea!"

"And what if you were writing about how you run up the stairs, hardly stopping to rest at all—and also about how your grandfather goes up the stairs! Let's start a poem like that." I wrote the two phrases below on chart paper, leaving a big space between each to fill in more poem about going up stairs.

I go up the stairs   My Grandfather
                       goes up the stairs

"Let's use just two words to tell how you go up the stairs and how your grandfather goes up the stairs. Two words: up and stop. What might the pattern be for you going up the stairs? What might it be for grandfather going up the stairs?"

It is wise to give them their instructions, show an example of what they're to do, and then to get them started by reading the poem aloud once more.

I don't collect their observations. The point of active engagement is to give them a chance to try this out right now before they forget it. The point isn't to collect and check their answers.

This could be the link, but I want to wedge a bit more teaching into this lesson.

I love this section of this minilesson. I'm hoping that by setting children up to use the earlier message that form should support meaning, I'm enabling these writers to comprehend that the patterns we design for our writing need to match and carry our meaning.

Of course this pattern is only one of many possible.

The children fill in a pattern of "Up/ up/ up/ stop. Up/ up/ up/ stop," for themselves and "Up/ stop/ stop/ stop. Up/ stop/ stop/ stop," for Grandfather.

Link

Ask children to come fetch you if they write in a pattern.

"The easiest way to write with patterns is to line things up, to keep rows the same." With my hands, I suggested rows. "See if any of you can do this today, and if you write in a pattern come and show me. Off you go."

MID-WORKSHOP TEACHING POINT

"Writers, may I stop you? I am seeing so many patterns. Listen to this poet, and you'll see that Maddie has written lists that end in twists." [*Fig. IX-1*]

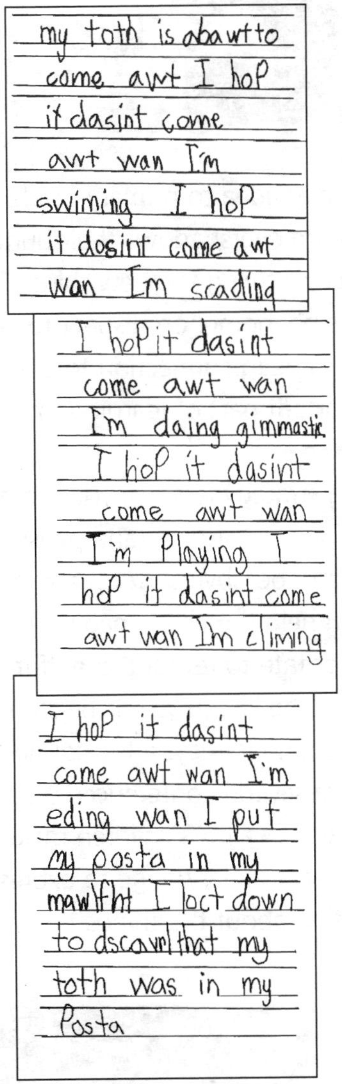

my toth is abautto come awt I hop it dasint come awt wan I'm swiming I hop it dosint come awt wan I'm scrading

I hoP it dasint come awt wan I'm daing gimmastic I hoP it dasint come awt wan I'm Playing I hoP it dasint come awt wan I'm climing

I hoP it dasint come awt wan I'm eding wan I put my posta in my mawtht I loct down to dscaver that my toth was in my Posta

Fig. IX-1   Maddie

My tooth is about to come out.
I hope it doesn't come out when I am swimming.
I hope it doesn't come out when I am skating.
I hope it doesn't come out when I am doing gymnastics.
I hope it doesn't come out when I am playing.
I hope it doesn't come out when I am climbing.
I hope it doesn't come out when I am eating.
When I put my pasta in my mouth
I looked down to discover
that my tooth was in my pasta.

TIME TO CONFER

Often when we introduce an idea to primary-grade children, they try it out with gusto. Sometimes their enthusiasm overshadows their purpose, though, and meaning flies out the window in service of trying the new thing. The idea of patterns in poems is a perfect candidate for this phenomenon. Expect to see several poems that use patterns but do not seem to have a deep connection to the writer. Remember that approximation is an important part of learning, and children approximate in different ways.

In conferences and strategy lessons, you are going to want to help children imagine alternate ways for the patterns (and physical layout, too) of their poems to convey meaning. This won't be obvious for many poems, so you may want to scan the text first to see if you can help the child imagine ways to do this. If you see possibilities for a child's text, don't hesitate to reveal those. If it's a poem about feeling lonely, the writer may want to isolate the line in which he stands alone at the window. If it's a poem about reoccurring thunder, maybe the sound needs to interrupt other words.

Be prepared to have several conferences that bring the writer back to the idea of topics that are both big and small. As children make decisions about the sound of their poems and the way they will use language to express themselves, they will need to be coached to continue writing about the things that matter most to them.

These conferences in *The Conferring Handbook* may be especially helpful today

- ▶ *"Can You Think of One Moment That Holds the Big Feeling the Ocean Gives You?"*
- ▶ *"Are Those the Sounds You Hear?"*

Also, if you have *Conferring with Primary Writers*, you may want to refer to the conferences in part seven.

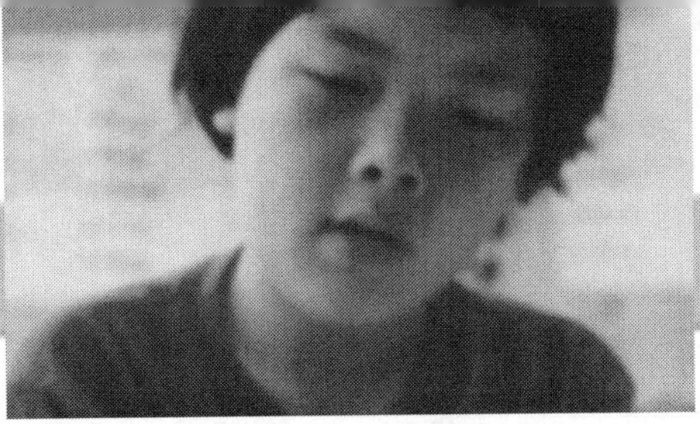

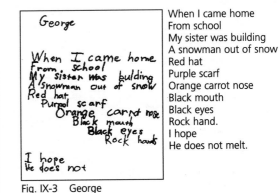

After-the-Workshop Share

Read and reread several poems that have patterns.

"Poems need to be read, reread, and reread. I'm going to end our workshop today by reading and rereading two poems. Listen to the patterns in these poems, and remember that poems, like weeks and weekends, days and nights, and like Sarah's necklace, have patterns." [*Figs. IX-2 and IX-3*]

Ask children to divide their poems into two categories: those that have patterns and those that don't. Ask them to consider adding patterns to those that don't have them.

"Turn, now, to your own poetry portfolio. Reread your poems and divide them into two piles: poems with patterns, and poems that don't yet have patterns. Then, tomorrow, consider revisiting the pile of poems that don't yet have patterns."

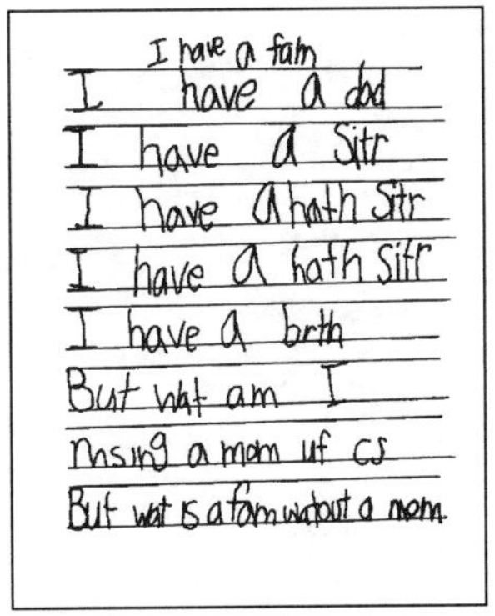

I have a family.
I have a dad.
I have a sister.
I have a half sister.
I have a half sister
I have a brother.
But what am I
Missing a mom of course
But what is a family without a mom.

Fig. IX-2   Consuela

When I came home
From school
My sister was building
A snowman out of snow
Red hat
Purple scarf
Orange carrot nose
Black mouth
Black eyes
Rock hand.
I hope
He does not melt.

Fig. IX-3   George

USING COMPARISONS TO CONVEY FEELINGS

GETTING READY

▶ "Inside My Heart" or another similar poem, written on chart paper
◉ See CD-ROM for resources

IF ONE OF YOUR GOALS IN THIS UNIT is to help children relish and play with language, then you're probably going to need to take the plunge into the deep water of figurative language. Because although it is true that poets seek out honest, precise words, that is true of all writers. Poets, more than other writers, use metaphor, simile, and personification to convey their meaning.

You may worry that these techniques are out of your children's reach, and you are probably right that the terms, definitions, and rules of figurative language could overburden a young child. But five- and six-year-olds have a special kinship with metaphor. The young child sees a leaf spin to the ground and says, "It's flying!" She notices an acorn with its shell still on and decides this is a magic elf. A wagon is an airplane, a line of chairs is a train, a pile of pots is a collection of kettledrums.

Make the most of this. Let children know that whereas one way to convey big feelings is by showing not telling, another way is by comparing the feelings to something else.

THE MINILESSON

Connection

Tell the children that you're glad they're putting feelings into their poems but that poets don't just "say them plain." They see feelings, like seashells, with fresh eyes.

"We've been talking about how poets find topics that give us big strong feelings, and I've noticed that many of you put those feelings into your poems. And I can see that you know that if you just write your feelings plain, like "I was mad," it sounds a little blah. We've learned that one way to convey feelings is by showing them, not telling them. Today I'll teach you another way to let readers know your feelings."

"Do you remember when we studied how Zoë saw the ceiling in a fresh way—as a sky—and she imagined the pencil sharpener had bees buzzing around inside it? And remember when we all tried to see our pine cones and our feathers with fresh eyes?"

"Well, today I'll show you a way to see *feelings* with fresh eyes too."

Teach

Tell the children that one way to put feelings into a poem is to say what the feelings are like. Show a poem in which the poet uses figurative language to convey a feeling.

"Sometimes we poets don't just *say* exactly how we feel; instead we say our feeling is *like* something else in the world. We compare our feelings to something

Annie Dillard once said of her writing, "I have all my Christmas tree ornaments but no Christmas tree." This has lingered with me. It is easy to use minilessons as a method for dumping doodads on kids. The problem is that no one can remember one hundred unrelated points. We can, however, remember particular bits of advice if they hang together. It's wise, then, to try to provide the Christmas tree as well as the ornaments in your minilessons.

Remember to use the exact same phrases you used earlier. If you try to say the same thing in different ways, some children won't comprehend that you are simply reiterating something you said earlier.

In this unit children are gently brought up the gradients of difficulty one small step at a time. We approach metaphor this way because we think this is an accessible avenue into figurative language.

else. Watch and listen as I reread part of this poem, "Inside My Heart," by Zoë. She wanted to write about how the things that happen in her life matter to her and make her heart full, but she didn't just want to say, 'Oh my heart is so full!' Instead, she made this poem show her feelings in a special, poetry-like way."

"She doesn't just come right out and tell us how she feels. She makes the poem say what she feels like by comparing her feelings to things in the world that remind her of that feeling."

Tell children the feeling the poet wanted to convey, and explain how the author wrote about things that hold that feeling.

"Instead of just saying how we feel, we poets *often* think of things in the world that remind us of that feeling and write about the thing to show the feeling. Dancing birds and wrestling puppies and laughing babies and birthday parties are all happy things in the world, and that's why Zoë chose them to describe the happy feeling in her heart."

Active Engagement

Ask the children to think of a time they felt sad, proud, angry, and so on. For each feeling, ask them to tell a partner what they'd say lives in their heart.

"Right now, right here, I want you poets to close down quietly for a minute or two. Will you think of a time recently when you felt really sad? If you were going to write about how *your* heart felt then, what kinds of things might you imagine to be living inside there?" I paused for a moment. "Tell your partner. Say it, 'Inside my heart lives . . .' and then say what lives there."

"Now, think about a particular time when you felt really proud. If you were going to write about how your heart felt then, what kinds of things might you imagine living in your heart?" Again, I paused for a moment. "Now say to your partner, 'Inside my heart lives. . . .'"

This is only one use for metaphor, but it's an accessible one so we begin here.

Inside My Heart
by Zoë Ryder White

Inside my heart lives
one birthday party
two jazz bands
three wrestling puppies
four dancing birds
five laughing babies
six blasting spaceships
seven lucky fireflies and
a sky full of stars.

Sometimes we're tempted to elicit the points we want to make by asking children a series of questions. I don't recommend this. If you have something to say, say it. Then let children's involvement come when they apply what you explicitly teach to their own lives, as in the upcoming active engagement.

When the content is as complex as it is, I reduce the complexity by giving children starting lines, carrying them into their approach to this work.

"Now, think of when you were angry. What lives in your heart?" This time after a minute of quiet, I again asked the children to turn and talk to their partners about what lives inside their hearts. This time, I listened in on some of the partnership conversations.

"I heard Henry say, 'In my heart there's a roaring lion.' That's beautiful. Why, when I am angry, my heart feels like a roaring lion, too."

Remind writers to speak with specifics.

"I love the way many of you are making your comparisons specific. You aren't saying 'I feel like a bird' but 'I feel like a bird in the blue, blue, sky.' Would you go back to your partner and make sure you were specific? Exactly when do you have the feeling? Is your comparison detailed?"

Link

Send the children off with the reminder that poets write about feelings in fresh ways. One such way is by using comparisons.

"So, poets, when you are writing or revising your writing today or any day, remember that poets try to write not only what we see but also what we feel in fresh ways. One way to do this is to write about the things in the world that remind us of that feeling. And remember to be specific. That's what Zoë did with the birthday party in her heart. Thumbs up if you think this is something you'll try today. Off you go!"

Obviously, this is more structured than usual. We don't usually give story starters or poem starters. But if this can jump-start our children into dabbling for a moment in figurative language, that seems wise.

The truth is that many of them probably are not yet making their comparisons specific. But this isn't a time for corrections and critique, so I give my coaching a positive twist.

At the end of the minilesson, it helps to try to show children how this minilesson builds on others. So, I remind children that the goal is to write about the world, and our feelings, in fresh ways . . . and tell them they now have several techniques for doing so. They can show instead of telling, they can recreate small moments, or they can use comparisons.

TIME TO CONFER

You may want to seek out some youngsters who, with a nudge from you, could sail with the concepts you taught today. You would be wise to confer with a few children who can end up mentoring the others. Look for the youngsters with rich imaginations. Go to the child who turns a stick into a wand, a laser, a wizard's cane.

The easiest way to teach figurative language (and the way that matches today's minilesson) is to help a writer convey a strong feeling by telling of a time he had that feeling. So if the child is describing when he had a hurt ankle and had to sit out the soccer game at recess, say, "Can you feel, right now, how sad and lonely you felt then? Show me how you sat when you were watching that game and couldn't join in. Can you try to get that feeling in you right now so you can write about it?"

When the child nods yes, press on. "Think of a whole other time in your life—a time when you're not even at school—when you felt that sad." Pause. Give him time. He'll probably come up with something. If that doesn't work, be more specific. "Can you get that sad feeling in you right now? Pretend you are feeling it now. You got it? Okay. Now help me feel that sad. Tell me about how your sad feeling feels. How sad was it? Sad like what? Like a broken stick, like a, a. . . ."

It was this sort of prompting that helped Henry write his poem. [*Fig. X-1*] Danielle's poem, however [*Fig. X-2*], spilled out as if by magic.

These conferences in *The Conferring Handbook* may be especially helpful today:

▶ *"Can You Think of One Moment That Holds the Big Feeling the Ocean Gives You?"*
▶ *"Are Those the Sounds You Hear?"*
▶ *"Can You Help Me See What You Saw?"*

Also, if you have *Conferring with Primary Writers*, you may want to refer to the conferences in part seven.

My pain is as
Tall as the
Empire state building.

Fig. X-1   Henry

Oh! I say.
Colored paint
in the sky.
It makes a
Rainbow.

Fig. X-2   Danielle

85

After-the-Workshop Share

Read children an example of a fresh comparison a writer in the class used.

"Writers, you're going to love this poem Evan wrote today! [*Fig. X-3*] He really thought of a way to tell us about his feelings that was new and interesting."

"Can you hear how he tells us the exact amount of lonely he was at the sleepover, even though he's also having a great time there? Evan decided that the best way to tell us the exact amount of loneliness he felt was to tell us how big it would be if we could see it. You know how our color tiles are one-inch squares? I guess one tile is about the size of how lonely Evan felt at the sleepover!"

Fig. X-3   Evan

"A Sleepover"
When we sat side by side
Having spaghetti
I wasn't lonely
When we tumbled around
Having a pillow fight
I wasn't lonely
Only 1 inch lonely

▶ Consider doing some shared writing. Perhaps it is a particularly beautiful day and you can bring the class outdoors to sit in the spring sunshine. "Let's get a feeling inside us. What should it be?" Maybe the class agrees that the spring sunshine makes them long for summer. "How can we show that longing feeling by comparing it to something else?" In such a fashion, you help the class combine efforts and write a poem.

▶ You could teach the class to reread their poems looking for feeling words that deserve development. Perhaps the poets will find words in their poems such as *fun* or *nice* or *happy* or *sad*. "Let's circle these words and try to really show our feelings by thinking about what they remind us of."

▶ Children can reread poems trying to find times when authors showed feelings by comparisons (by metaphor), such as "Love Don't Mean" by Eloise Greenfield.

Today's minilesson will have lit up the whole landscape of figurative language, and you will definitely want to bring all your children's work home to study what they have done. Be prepared. Expect unpredictable, astonishing results. Some students who have always been very competent writers will surprise you by seeming to have lead feet when it comes to metaphor, and others who may struggle when asked to write long, sequential texts will take your breath away. [*Fig. X-4*]

You won't want to miss seeing their flights of fancy. Dr. Spock always advises parents, "Catch your child in the act of doing something good." That's crucial advice for teachers of figurative language as well. You can't really lay out steps 1, 2, and 3 a child should take to see the world through the lens of metaphor. But you can invite comparisons and then be ready to celebrate any small or grand fireworks you see on the page.

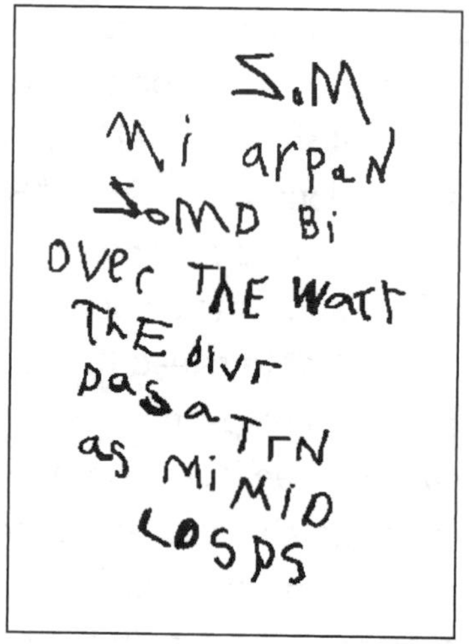

```
SoM
Mi arpaN
SoMD Bi
Over THE watr
THE divr
Dasa TrN
as MiMID
LoSPS
```

Zoom
My airplane
Zooms by
Over the water
The driver
Does a turn
As my mind
Loops

Fig. X-4   Jaques

CONTRASTING ORDINARY AND POETIC LANGUAGE

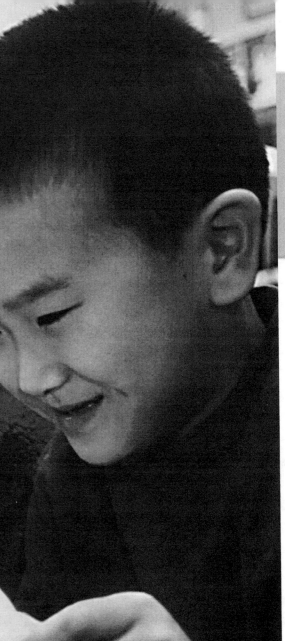

GETTING READY

▶ A two-column chart: one column titled Ordinary Language, the other titled Poetic Language. In the Ordinary Language column, list typical sentences from your or your children's writing that describe something everyone in the room has experienced. On the Poetic Language side, rework each sentence to incorporate figurative language. After the first three or four examples, leave the right-hand column blank, so you can elicit ideas from your children.

⊙ See CD-ROM for resources

YOU'VE RECENTLY ENCOURAGED YOUR CHILDREN *to take on the language of poetry. They will have only just begun to use metaphor and simile consciously and will need lots more time and more encouragement. Many people will tell you that the best time to learn a new language is when you are very young, and this is as true for poetic language as for Spanish or Arabic. But your youngsters will need time to approximate. Earlier you made a great point of appreciating their invented spellings. "Just spell it as best you can," you said to them. Now you'll want to be equally supportive of their invented simile and metaphor. "Just describe things the best you can," you'll say.*

In this minilesson, you'll again encourage children to reach for brand new ways to convey ideas and images that don't fit into ordinary language. Yesterday your point was that poets don't always come straight out and say what they are feeling. Instead, poets sometimes show their feelings by saying of what they are reminded.

Your point will be that poets reach for powerful ways to show lots of things, not just feelings. A poet may use comparisons to convey a sound, an image, an observation, an idea—or almost anything!

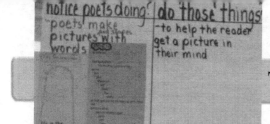

THE MINILESSON

Connection

Remind writers that poets don't just say the feeling, they find something to which to compare the feeling. Give examples from children's work.

"Yesterday we discovered that if a poet wants to show she is happy, she doesn't always come right out and say she's happy. Instead she may say something like, 'In my heart there's a birthday party and two laughing babies.' So yesterday when Greg wanted to write that he felt lonely at camp, he wrote, 'When I went to sleep, I felt like I was an orphan.' And Jesse wanted to say she was happy to have an éclair in her lunch box, so she said, 'My lunch made today feel like Christmas.'"

Tell the children that poets use comparison as a way to show not only feelings but almost anything important.

"When we write poems, we don't just reach for ways to show *our feelings*, we also need to reach for ways to help readers picture and experience whatever we see and experience. Today I'm going to show you how poets compare *whatever* we're writing about (not just our feelings) to something else."

In at least half of your minilessons, you begin by summarizing the previous day's work and by sharing an example or two generated by children who did this work well. These examples make particular children famous for their work with language and give children models that are within their grasp.

Then your connection turns a bend, as this one does, and you name what you will teach today that can help writers not just today but everyday. Ideally you show how today's lesson builds on lessons from other days.

Teach

Unveil the chart contrasting ordinary and poetic language.

"Let me show you how ordinary language goes, and how poetic language goes:"

ORDINARY LANGUAGE	POETIC LANGUAGE
The kids kept jumping up to say more ideas.	Ideas popcorned about the classroom.
When I get to school early the classroom is quiet.	When I get to school early, the classroom is asleep.
The sky is blue.	The sky is like a blue ocean.
When I draw, I make pictures of dragons and castles.	Castles and dragons live in my pencil.
The clouds are puffy and white.	
The wind makes the classroom door shut loudly.	
We line up to go down the hall.	

"Do you see how I can take ordinary language and rewrite it in a fresh way by comparing? When one of you and then another of you jumps up with ideas, I can say, 'Ideas popcorned around the room,' but your ideas aren't *really* popcorn. And when the room is quiet, I *can say* the classroom is sleeping, but it isn't *really* asleep."

I retain as many things as possible between one version and the next, altering the phrases only to include figurative language. You'll see throughout this series of units that when I want to highlight an aspect or feature of writing, I often show the same bit of writing without the feature or aspect and then with it. This only works if the before and after versions are kept absolutely similar except for the one feature I'm hoping to spotlight. That is, if I want to say that descriptions are more effective if they include sensory details and my 'before' version shows me sitting on my front stoop watching people walk along the sidewalk, my next version can't be of me sitting in the park! If only two old people walk along the sidewalk in my 'before' version, the same two people—and only them—need to be there in the 'after' version.

Active Engagement

Ask the children, with their partners, to continue producing poetic version of ordinary phrases. Collect children's ideas and use them to complete the chart.

"Let's try some of these together. Can you and your partner work on the parts of the chart I haven't filled in?"

Ordinary Language	Poetic Language
The kids kept jumping up to say more ideas.	Ideas popcorned about the classroom.
When I get to school early the classroom is quiet.	When I get to school early, the classroom is asleep.
The sky is blue.	The sky is like a blue ocean.
When I draw, I make pictures of dragons and castles.	Castles and dragons live in my pencil.
The clouds are puffy and white.	The clouds are like marshmallows. The clouds are like blobs of whipped cream. There are ice cream clouds in the sky.
The wind makes the classroom door shut loudly.	The wind slams the classroom door. The door crashes closed like a drum.
We line up to go down the hall.	We line up like a choo-choo train. We snake down the hall.

"Wow, look at all these exciting ways we have found to say what we want to say! Comparing things is such a powerful tool in poetry."

Link

Remind the children that whenever they write, they can use comparisons to help readers understand.

"Whenever you write—and especially whenever you write poetry—if you want readers to really feel and see and hear what you are saying, one thing you can do is to use comparisons. If you want to try this, and feel like you need extra help, stay on the rug. The rest of you, get going."

This active engagement gives children lots of repeated practice saying things poetically. Be sure to let children work with partners so that every child has a chance to do this as best he or she can. If you bypass this phase and instantly begin to elicit suggestions from the whole group, a large percentage of the class will just sit back and let others do the work (and gain the practice).

The remaining phrases (the ones I didn't do already) can be rewritten using figurative language fairly easily. My goal is to set children up for success.

Obviously you could list many more possibilities, but you'll quickly make your point. It's time for children to write.

This is a common and very effective way to make your instruction multilevel. Some teachers frequently say, "If you need extra help, stay on the rug. The rest of you, get started."

You'll probably want to pull together a small group of children and help them practice making metaphors. If you gather on the carpet, start with the carpet. "So let me show you what I mean about how poets compare. I'm just looking at this blue carpet and I'm thinking, I could compare it to—a sea! Our carpet is like the sea, and we're what? Could we say that pulled together like this, on the carpet, we're an island of talk? Or. . . ."

"You can do the same with your pencil. So, watch me write and think, 'What can we compare the pencil to?' When I write, it's like my pencil is . . . ? What?"

Try to be ready to go with whatever children invent. You'll want to support their approximations, knowing they'll grow into this over time. After a bit of small-group practice, you might ask the children to get out whatever poems they worked on yesterday. Then you could quickly scan the pile and see if one seems promising. Look for a poem that addresses a subject many of the kids know. Then ask all the small-group members to help the writer imagine how he could bring some "comparing" into his poem.

Only after this would you set each child up to try this in his or her poems. You'll find some children, like Denise, stay pretty literal. [*Fig. XI-1*] Don't worry that this isn't overly creative. If a child says only, "The moon is like the sun," try to draw out what it is that they both do.

In her poem [*Fig. XI-2*], Samantha makes two different comparisons. You could help her sustain one comparison rather than pile two up against each other.

These conferences in *The Conferring Handbook* may be especially helpful today:

- "*Can You Think of One Moment That Holds the Big Feeling the Ocean Gives You?*"
- "*Are Those the Sounds You Hear?*"
- "*Can You Help Me See What You Saw?*"

Also, if you have *Conferring with Primary Writers*, you may want to refer to the conferences in part seven.

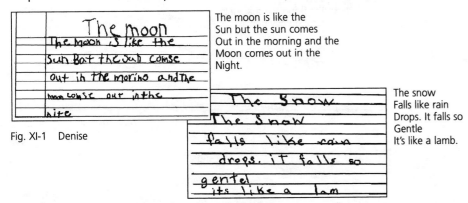

The moon is like the
Sun but the sun comes
Out in the morning and the
Moon comes out in the
Night.

Fig. XI-1   Denise

The snow
Falls like rain
Drops. It falls so
Gentle
It's like a lamb.

Fig. XI-2 Samantha

Show an example of a child who used "comparing" in a poem.

"You guys, David did such an interesting thing in his poetry today. He definitely compared, but he did it in a really neat way. Let me read you his poem." [*Fig. XI-3*]

"Did you hear how he compared sitting in his desk chair to flying in space? First he was sitting in his chair and then, all of a sudden, he was flying a spaceship! He didn't have to tell us he was just pretending to fly the ship, or that he was imagining himself flying. Instead, he just said, 'I'm flying the spaceship.'"

Ask the children to share their work with a partner and to find something interesting their partner did with language.

"Would each of you share your work with your partner, and find something interesting your partner did with language?"

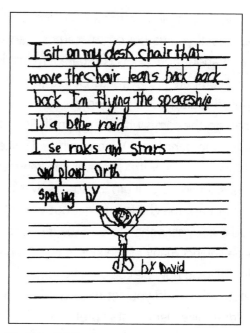

Fig. XI-3   David

I sit on my desk chair
That moves
The chair leans
Back, back
Back
I'm flying the spaceship
It's a bumpy ride
I see rocks and stars
And planet Earth
Speeding by

- Invite children to search picture books and poems they know for comparisons (or metaphor, if you use that term). For example, "Time of Wonder," by Robert McClosky is full of them: "In the quiet of the night one hundred pairs of eyes are watching you . . . the moon comes out, making a rainbow . . . a promise that the storm will be over soon . . . the wind whispers a lullaby. . . ." You could read books aloud and children could signify by thumbs up that they just heard a comparison.
- You may want children to go on a search for times when poems from earlier this year used comparisons to show something.
- You can remind children that early in the unit, Zoë described a pencil sharpener as holding bees that buzz and the ceiling as "like the sky." "We've labeled our classroom with ordinary language: blocks, library, math. Maybe we could rethink our labels and this time use poetic language." Of course, some new things will now merit labels: the seashell, the plant, the eraser, the door to the classroom.
- You could suggest that the class live like poets. "Let's just carry on our lives, doing what we do, but then I'll say stop, and we'll try to use poetic language to name what we're doing."

Poetic Language	Compares What to What?
Fireworks burst into bloom The lonely sky 　　　　　—Rebecca	Fireworks to flowers The empty sky to a lonely person
There are bees inside the pencil sharpener	Grinding of pencil to bees buzzing
The ceiling is the sky for the classroom	Ceiling to sky
Inside my heart lives a birthday party 　　　—Zoë Ryder White	Happiness to a birthday in one's heart
Closed, it sleeps On its side Quietly, The silver Image Of some Small fish 　　　—Valerie Worth	Safety pin to fish on its side
My teacher opens *My Father's Dragon* and I'm flying on the back of a dragon 　　　—Lucus	Reading to flying on back of dragon
Moon is like a D 　　　—Klara	The moon to alphabet letters

You'll definitely want to use the rubric you developed at the start of this unit to guide you as you look over your children's work. Don't wait until the end of the unit to do this! Remember that no one poem needs to contain all things. You'll look at the child's portfolio of work and think about what you have seen children doing. Notice how many children show evidence that they've learned to write by ear, adjusting their poems so they "sound right." Their ears needn't guide them as yours would. The key thing isn't that you agree that their poem sounds 'right.' Instead, the key thing is that they are attuned to the sounds of language as they draft and revise poems. Notice their attentiveness to language. Be sure that you ask children to join you in looking for evidence of these and other goals. You may, for example, decide to ask every child to reread his or her poems and to leave sticky notes in places that demonstrate that they've worked hard to make their poems "sound good." You could do the same thing for other goals you've tried to teach.

STRETCHING OUT A COMPARISON (SUSTAINING A METAPHOR)

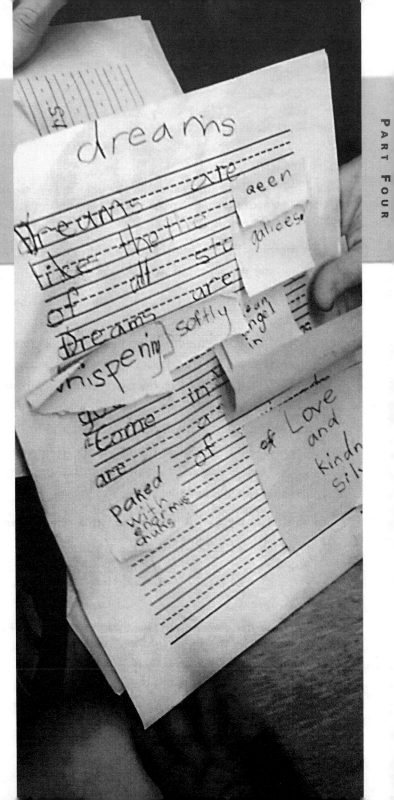

GETTING READY

▸ Comparison chart from the previous session

● See CD-ROM for resources

WHEN YOU PLAN A UNIT OF STUDY, *it's not hard to generate a nice long list of possible topics that fit under the unit umbrella. There are zillions of things very young children could learn about almost any aspect of writing.*

The challenge is to plan a learning journey that enables them not only to hear about topics but also to approach, experiment with, develop, and extend a few skills. Resist the temptation to turn your study of poetic language into a vocabulary course. Of course you could throw lots of terms at children—personification, simile, and the rest—but you might end up taking away the children's finesse and comfort with this new language, making them as anxious and rule bound as the rest of us.

The decision to avoid overwhelming children with a lot of terms and definitions is not, however, a decision against rigor. But real rigor comes from taking what one does and thinking, "How could this be done even better?"

In this minilesson, you'll teach children to stay with, develop, and sustain their comparisons. This teaching will make it less likely that their writing contains a hodge-podge of very mixed metaphors. You'll show children that just as they can take one moment in time and stretch it out across a sequence of pages, so too can they take a comparison and stretch it out across a sequence of lines in a poem.

THE MINILESSON

Connection

Remind your children that earlier in the year they learned to write about small moments, stretching them across several pages.

"I have something really, really important to teach you, and it's something that children usually learn in college, not in first grade! But I think you are so smart as poets you may be able to understand. So listen really carefully."

"Do you remember, when we were learning about writing small moments, we stretched out our moments across a few pages? We didn't just write, 'I said goodbye to my friend and she moved,' but instead we said, 'I stood outside my friend's apartment and thought how this would be my last day at this door. Then I knocked. She came to the door. "Bye," I said. "Bye," she said. And we looked at each other. Then she moved away.'"

"Remember how we stretched that one tiny goodbye moment out so it lasted across many pages?"

Tell them that today they'll learn to stretch a comparison across many lines.

"Well today I want to teach you that if you compare in your poem, it's really smart to stretch that comparing out across many lines."

Teach

Refer to the earlier comparison chart. Tell the children if you wrote a poem about one of the items on the chart, you wouldn't want to write it so the comparison lasted only one line. Show such a poem.

"So let's go back to the chart of comparisons we made yesterday. If I write a poem about this one—'When I get to school, the classroom is sleeping'—I *could* go like this:"

You might want to leaf through a stack of minilessons and notice all the ways teachers have for saying, "Kids, listen up." This is a new way to call for children's attention—but it works!

The pattern in your minilessons is that you first remind children of the work they have already been doing. Often this means saying, "Yesterday. . . ." But many minilessons build upon the foundation of work from earlier in the year. I have decided in this instance that if children recall how they stretched out and sustained (elongated) their retelling of a small moment, this could help them grasp the concept of sustaining their metaphor. So my connection doesn't harken back to yesterday but instead, to the lessons that are foundational to today's point.

I could also have begun with stretching out words to hear their sounds, then talked about stretching stories across a sequence of pages, and only later emphasized stretching a metaphor ("a comparison") across the lines of a poem. Either way, I'd be reminding children of what they already know, then taking only a small step into new terrain.

> **First Version**
>
> **Mornings**
>
> **I come in**
>
> **The classroom is sleeping.**
>
> **I push chairs in and straighten tables.**
>
> **Then the kids come.**

For expediency's sake, I had this version already written. I'd written a very brief poem that doesn't illustrate a host of extraneous aspects of poetry. Because I plan to contrast this version of a poem with another version in which I sustain the comparison (the metaphor), I keep the two versions similar except for the one difference that I'm highlighting (fleeting versus sustaining references to the metaphor).

"In my poem, I just quickly mention the idea that the classroom is asleep. I compare the classroom to a sleeping person but I do that comparing quickly," My gesture suggested I dart in and out, "on just one line. The comparison isn't in the first line," I pointed to that line on my poem, "it *is* in the second line," again I pointed, "it isn't in the third or the fourth line."

Write another version of this poem in front of the children, sustaining the metaphor and thinking aloud as you go.

"So I'm going to try to rewrite this poem and stay with the idea that the classroom is sleeping. Okay, help me with this. I am remembering when I get to school very early and the classroom is totally quiet, like it is sleeping. I am thinking of all the things I do in the sleeping classroom that are similar to what I'd do if the classroom were a sleeping person. Hmm, let me think about when people are sleeping. I'm thinking about how we tiptoe and go, 'Shush.' Okay, so now I'll try my poem again and try to stretch out how I compare the classroom to a sleepy morning."

First Version	**New Version**
Mornings	**Mornings**
I come in	**I tiptoe in quietly**
The classroom is sleeping.	**The classroom is sleeping.**
I push chairs in and straighten tables.	**I ease the chairs into their spots, careful not to bang them. I lift, not push, the tables to straighten them.**
Then the kids come.	**I'm careful to let the classroom sleep. Then the kids clang, clatter, bang in And wake up the room.**

"Do you see how, on many lines, I kept up the idea of the sleeping classroom? How'd I do that in line one? Listen again," I reread line one, "'I tiptoe in.' Why?" The children talked about this for a minute. "You are smart. I tiptoe so as to not wake up the sleeping classroom!" In this fashion, I continued to discuss the new version of the poem.

Active Engagement

Involve the kids in writing a second parallel version, again using a comparison from the chart.

"Let's try to stretch out another comparison together. Let's take this one from our chart: 'We line up like a train.' We *could* just stretch out the story." I pointed to the first version I had quickly written:

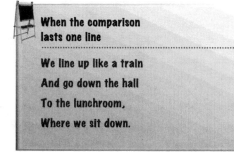

When the comparison lasts one line

We line up like a train
And go down the hall
To the lunchroom,
Where we sit down.

"But we could also try to *stretch out* the way we compare our line of kids to a train. Remember how I did this before in the sleeping classroom poem? That time, I thought, 'I need to remember when I get to school early and the room is quiet,' and I thought, 'How can I say that I come into the classroom in the same way that I'd go into a bedroom where someone is sleeping?'"

"So now you need to remember when we line up to go down the hall and it's like we're a train, and you and your partner need to think of ways that what we do, going down the hall, is like a train. Talk about that."

My last instructions propelled them into the conversation I wanted them to have. I listened in on Aidan and Khalea.

Aidan: "We could say we buy tickets."

Khalea: "But we don't buy tickets!"

The teaching component of the minilesson always employs a method of teaching. In this minilesson, the method is demonstration. What are the qualities of an effective demonstration? Among other things, the teacher needs to begin at the beginning and proceed through the sequence of activities step by step (not simply talk about them). It helps to speak your thoughts as the demonstration proceeds so children can almost look inside your mind and see what's going on.

Notice that I let children in on the sequence of considerations that I ponder as I go about the step-by-step process of trying to sustain my metaphor.

Aidan: "We could say our teacher says, 'All aboard,' so we line up like a train."

Khalea: "And go chug-chug, chug-chug to the next stop."

Aidan: "We could say that you call, 'All aboard,' and we line up like a train and then choo-choo down the hall to the next stop."

"Okay, so far we have this." Alongside the first version, I wrote the version Aidan dictated:

When the comparison lasts one line	When the comparison stretches across many lines
We line up like a train	"All aboard!"
And go down the hall	We line up like a train
To the lunchroom,	And choo-choo down the hall
Where we sit down.	To the next stop,
	The lunchroom.

Soon the class had decided the last line could be, "Where we get off the train and eat hot dogs."

Link

Ask poets to look at the poems they wrote the day before and notice if they made comparisons. If so, could they stretch these out across lines?

"Would you each look at the poem you worked on yesterday? Read it over and think, 'Am I comparing one thing to another?' If you have done some comparing, thumbs up. Okay, partners, will you look at these comparing poems and think how you could stretch out the comparing, like we did here with the sleeping classroom and the train-like line. Once you have an idea for what to do, you can get started."

The beauty of having eavesdropped on partner talks is you have a way to rescue the conversation. If one child produces a response that dead-ends conversation, you have the option of calling on someone who can save the day!

You'll want to practice this yourself. Earlier, Danielle suggested a rainbow is like colored paint in the sky. If you wanted to extend that metaphor, consider how you could do so. Think of what you know about colored paintings that could be linked to a rainbow. Perhaps you realize that paintings are the work of an artist. Who is the artist responsible for this rainbow? Perhaps you think that colored paintings are sometimes framed. Is the rainbow framed by anything? Mountains? Tree tops? This is the process writers go through as we try to extend our metaphors.

Mid-Workshop Teaching Point

Ask the children to help someone in the class stretch a comparison.

"Writers, may I stop you? Paul would love some of your help. He's written a poem about cats [*Fig. XII-1*], and he does lots of comparing."

"Paul did some smart work today. He realized he didn't stretch his comparing across the lines of his poem—one line compares a cat to a mouse, one to a stuffed animal, one to a wish. So he decided to just compare a cat with a stuffed animal. But now he is worried that his poem will be awfully short. Could you and your partner talk and see if you can give ideas for how to stretch out his comparisons?"

The room was filled with talk. Soon I reconvened the class and gathered their suggestions.

"Tell how you sleep with your cat like she is a teddy bear."

"Tell that she is hairy like a stuffed animal."

Remind writers to stretch comparisons with their own writing.

"So I'm hoping some of you, like Paul, are stretching your comparing out across several lines of your poem."

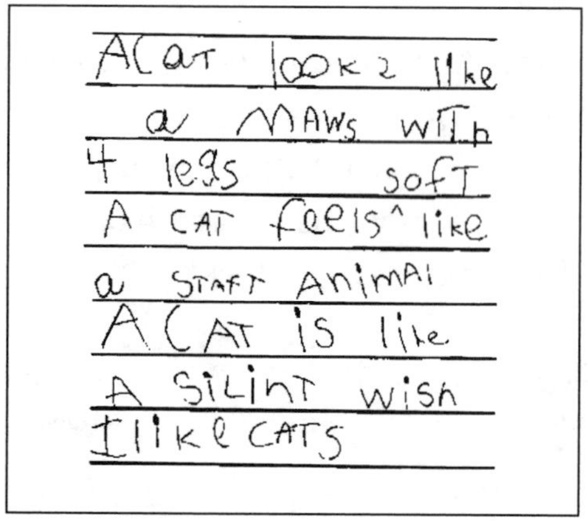
ACat lookz like
a maws with
4 legs soft
A cat feels^ like
a staft animal
A Cat is like
A silint wish
I like cats

Fig. XII-1 Paul

A cat looks like a mouse
With four legs.
A cat feels soft like a
Stuffed animal.
A cat is like a silent wish.
I like cats.

TIME TO CONFER

Although the unit of study is on poetry, you'll want to be sure your conferences support children's general development as writers. You'll want to spend some time, usually in the middle of the unit, focusing on children who need special support with spelling. Notice whether children are spelling long, challenging words in chunks rather than letter by letter. The words they automatically know should give them lots of word power, but you may need to teach children to think, "What words do I know that can help me with *this* word?"

You may notice that a group of your children are misspelling a certain chunk—perhaps an ending—in similar ways. Are many of them spelling the ending *ly* as *le*? If you see a group of children who could profit from similar help, pull them together. Tell them what you have noticed. Ask them to reread, searching for places where they made the error and to fix those places. (This will give them repeated practice.) Suggest they work together to list words they *might* use that have the spelling pattern.

These conferences in *The Conferring Handbook* may be especially helpful today:

- ▶ *"Can You Think of One Moment That Holds the Big Feeling the Ocean Gives You?"*
- ▶ *"Are Those the Sounds You Hear?"*
- ▶ *"Can You Help Me See What You Saw?"*

Also, if you have *Conferring with Primary Writers*, you may want to refer to the conferences in part seven.

Read children an example of an extended comparison from one of their classmates.

"As I was walking around today, I came across Amanda doing some exciting work. She was writing a poem about the stapler, and she was in the middle of making some changes. See, she had been comparing the stapler to a shark, and then later to an alligator. As she reread, she decided to make her comparison all about one thing." [*Fig. XII-2*]

Fig. XII-2   Amanda

The stapler
Opens its mouth
And closes its
Mouth
It snaps
An alligator
Keeping my ideas
Together

This minilesson will probably not make a lasting difference for every child in your classroom. Your teaching needs to be multilevel, and with this session, chances are good that only children who take easily to metaphor will grasp what you've tried to teach. But you will have exposed others to a concept that is very important, and a year or two from now, they'll revisit this and it'll suddenly make sense.

Meanwhile, however, you may want to extend this work just a bit. Do so through conferences and strategy lessons with children who seem interested and perhaps through another minilesson (but not more—don't continue too long with a concept that may be over the heads of many of your kids).

Your children may understand the idea of stretching a comparison (adults call this sustaining metaphor) throughout a poem more fully if they study examples from published poetry. The following poem sustains comparisons beautifully. Before you read the poem, tell children that in the poem a cow is likened to a mountain. Ask kids to generate a few images of a mountain. Join in to be sure they generate a list of images that'll pay off when they read the poem. ("A mountain has peaks and is rocky . . . sometimes the rocks get loose and roll thump, thump down.") Then you could ask children in pairs to hunt for ways in which this author keeps her comparison up across many lines.

If a few children revise their poems to stretch out their comparisons, you can show version one and then version two. Children can notice what the young author already did to stretch out the comparing (which may include realizing they'd jammed too many comparisons side by side into one poem) and perhaps help the author stretch out the comparing even more.

cow
by Valerie Worth

The cow
Coming
Across the grass
Moves
Like a mountain
Toward us;
Her hipbones
Jut
Like sharp
Peaks
Of stone,
Her hoofs
Thump
Like dropped
Rocks:
Almost
Too late
She stops

FINDING TREASURES IN DISCARDED DRAFTS

GETTING READY

▶ All the children's poetry folders

▶ A revision folder for each child

▶ Overheads (or charts with enlarged copies) of a few poems that one child in the class has chosen to discard

● See CD-ROM for resources

THIS SESSION MARKS THE FINAL BEND *in the road of this study. Although the unit could continue for weeks, it's time to head toward publication. You'll ask children to reread their work again, separating their poems into piles. You'll remind students that very often, hidden in the midst of a bad poem will be a brilliant, original, deeply true line. You'll invite students to rummage through their trash piles, looking for lines—even phrases—around which they can conceivably write wonderful new poems. Often, all that a poet needs is one line. Annie Dillard writes about this in* The Writing Life:

> *It is handed to you, but only if you look for it. . . . One line of a poem, the poet said—only one line, but Thank God for that one line—drops from the ceiling. Thornton Wilder cited this unnamed writer of sonnets: one line of a sonnet falls from the ceiling, and you tap in the others around it with a jeweler's hammer. (1989, 75–76)*

In this session you'll suggest that sometimes in the midst of a not very special poem, we find a phrase or a line or an image that deserves to be kept, and from this, we write new poems.

THE MINILESSON

Connection

Tell the children you've seen signs of spring—that the world seems to be getting ready for a party. Suggest it might be time to plan their celebration.

"Poets, I was walking to school today and on the corner by the church, I saw that the crocuses are out. And then I saw that down by the playground fence, the forsythia are starting to bloom. I got this feeling that the whole world is signaling to us that it's going to be time, soon, for a celebration."

"Do you think we could begin planning for our poetry celebration?"

Remind the children that this means they need to shift full speed into revision.

"If we want to publish next Friday (and I think we could), then we need to shift into revision starting today. We'll need to begin right now doing some serious work finding the poems that deserve to be published."

Suggest that each child go off alone and reread everything he or she has written, culling out the poems that deserve to be revised. (This interrupts the minilesson.)

"So before I carry on with this minilesson, let's give ourselves ten minutes of total silence while we each reread every poem we've written and put the ones we like best—the ones that deserve to be revised—into our revision folders. You can stay here on the carpet or go back to your seats, but we need total silence as you make decisions. You'll want to find at least four or five poems that have promise and that deserve to be revised. I'll bring you your revision folders as you work."

Teach

Reconvene the class. Liken their discarded poems to the town dump and tell about salvaging treasures at the dump. Ask them to search for lines that are treasures in their pile of discarded poems.

"Poets, I see most of you are done. Can we gather again?"

"Okay, now before we go any further, I want to talk to you about the poems you have in your reject pile."

If you're noticing that this isn't a normal introduction, you're right. But that's the point. The goal is to make today stand out. The goal is to create a sense of occasion. Even though by now the children have had lots of celebrations, it's still important to try to wrap each one in a special aura.

I'm breaking the normal pattern in yet a second way. Instead of giving the minilesson and then sending children off to work, I give them one set of directions, send them off to do just that, and then reconvene them for the real minilesson. I know if I try to teach them to do steps 1, 2, and 3, then launch them into step 1, my directions for steps 2 and 3 will get lost.

"Have you ever been to a big huge town dump? When I was a child, our town had a dump. Everyone brought trash there every week. I used to love to go with my Dad. While he made trips between the car and the mountain of refuse, I'd pick around in the trash and find all these cool things."

"So while my dad carried trash from the car to the dump, I'd carry treasures from the dump to the car! I love finding treasures in the trash. Has anyone here ever done that?"

"Today, and often when you write, remember that if you look hard, you can find little treasures in writing that is mostly trash."

Give an example of a child in the class who had decided to discard a poem but then found something in that poem that made it worth revising.

"For example, Sarah told me yesterday that she didn't like this poem—that it didn't deserve to be revised." [*Fig. XIII-1*]

"But I told her, 'Look again. Maybe there is a line or a word that you *do* like! And sure enough. She circled the phrase, 'my mom comes home late.'"

"So then I told her that what I do is, I take whatever I *do* like and I write it on top of a new page. Sometimes I can make a new poem out of it. Look at what Sarah wrote next." [*Fig. XIII-2*]

If I'd simply told children to reread their rejected drafts looking for bits they could salvage, I don't think I'd have tapped their sense of adventure. But I suspect many children identify with my childhood delight at picking through the mounds of trash at the town dump, spotting really grand stuff, and carrying it off to my dad's car. And because I've used the image of picking through the town dump to recruit children's energy, I suspect they'll eagerly search through their rejected drafts for stuff they can salvage.

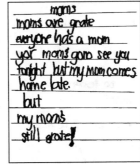

Fig. XIII-1 Sarah

"Moms"
Moms are great
Everyone has a mom
Your mom's going to see you
Tonight but my mom comes
Home late
But my mom's still great

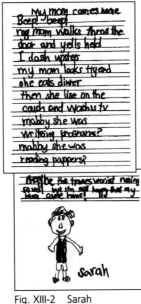

Fig. XIII-2 Sarah

"My Mom Comes Home Late"
Beep! Beep!
My mom walks through the door
And yells
Hello!
I dash upstairs
My mom looks tired
She eats dinner then she
Lies on the couch and
Watches TV
Maybe she was writing programs?
Maybe she was reading papers?
But maybe the trains
Weren't running so well?
I'm still happy that my mom came home!

Active Engagement

Ask the class to help one child look through his discarded poems, listening for lines or phrases they think deserve more attention.

"Would you help Leo look through his 'trash pile'? I've made overheads of some of the poems he thinks aren't good. I'm going to read a few to you and show them on the overhead, and will you listen for whether you hear a line, a phrase, you think deserves to be salvaged, to be saved?" I did this, and the children talked with their partners. Finally, as a class, we identified a great line.

"So Leo, what you might want to do is to write this line on a new paper, like Sarah did, and see if you can grow a new poem."

Link

Tell the class that they may want to look through their own pile of discarded poems before they start the work of revision.

"Today, before you begin to revise the poems you love, some of you may want to pick through *your* trash pile. Expect to find some treasures. Remember this advice is not only for today but for *whenever* you write."

You'll notice that Stephanie and I don't hesitate to use words that her first graders may not understand. We are careful, however, to surround those words with enough context that they'll be meaningful to children. One example of this came earlier in this minilesson when I described the pile of refuse at the dump. Here I talk about salvaging good bits of poems.

TIME TO CONFER

You'll probably want to use this minilesson as an excuse to help a few children who haven't yet written a lot of strong poems make one, last effort to produce something. Sometimes the excitement of an upcoming celebration can make all the difference.

If a child has one good line, you may want to teach the child to reread that line with reverence. I find when I want to write well, I need to be moved by my own writing. Help the child get goosebumps from his or her own writing, and this will put the child on the right road. Remember too that all writing thrives on detail and honesty.

Meanwhile, you may want to help children who are refining already nice poems use published poems as examples. The work you did earlier noticing and naming strategies Angela Johnson used can be recalled now. Children may notice the conventions of poetry, including the fact that most parts capitalize the first letter in every line. Children may study titles of poems. Some are labels, some are the same as the first line. The real point will be for children to realize they can study exemplar texts and then incorporate what they learn into their own writing.

These conferences in *The Conferring Handbook* may be especially helpful today:

▶ *"Can You Think of One Moment That Holds the Big Feeling the Ocean Gives You?"*

▶ *"Are Those the Sounds You Hear?"*

▶ *"Can You Help Me See What You Saw?"*

Also, if you have *Conferring with Primary Writers*, you may want to refer to the conferences in part seven.

AFTER-THE-WORKSHOP SHARE

Ask the children to share one not-great poem with a treasure in it.

"You all did some interesting thinking today, and I'd really like for you to see as much of it as I got to see. When you come to the rug today to share, bring one poem you *thought* you wanted to throw away but then decided to hold on to. Be ready to share with the class your reason or reasons for saving it."

"Carlos found a pattern he loved in his poem, and he added lines to make the pattern show! Listen:" [*Fig. XIII-3*]

Much of the time we use the share as an opportunity to highlight the work of one or two children, as we teach the rest of the class from these few solid examples. Sometimes, however, the share is a great time to make public the many kinds of effective and productive work that were happening in the class that day. In this kind of share, we can help children be more creative in the ways they approach their own writing.

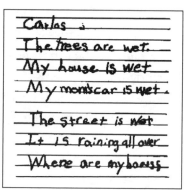

Fig. XIII-3   Carlos

The trees are wet.
My house is wet.
My mom's car is wet.

The street is wet.
It is raining all over.
Where are my boots?

ASSESSMENT

Take home the poems your children have selected as worthy of revision and reread them, asking, "Of all that I could teach at this point, what would help the most?" Your next minilesson (like all your minilessons) will grow from your assessment.

You'll no doubt find one or two ideas for strategies that the class could benefit from learning, but you'll also see that four children need one thing, another group needs another. Plan out the strategy lessons you'll give tomorrow. You could use the minilesson from Session XIV as a strategy lesson instead. Another possible topic might be that it is very important for poems to make sense and that revision can involve asking someone to read our writing and tell us what they glean from it. Then, too, some poems will be about abstract concepts like love and friendship; usually these poems will benefit from being more concrete.

Use your conferring guide sheet to help you see what children can do, can almost but not quite do, and what they can't yet do. You'll want your teaching to focus especially on what seems within grasp of your children.

CONTRASTING POEMS WITH STORIES

GETTING READY

▶ Two versions of a child's work on chart paper: one written as a story, the other as a poem (an example from your own class or the example in this lesson)

▶ Single special paper clip for each child for the share

● See CD-ROM for resources

IN THIS SESSION, YOU'LL HELP YOUR CHILDREN *revise their poems. To prepare for this, you will have looked over the poems they hope to revise and publish, thinking, "What can I say that'll help the most?" You will probably be amazed at the variety of poems your children have written. Although the variety is heartening, it also means that there won't be a small cluster of revision strategies that every child can use with every poem. Instead, children will need to categorize their poems, handling different kinds of drafts differently.*

In this session, you help children turn story-like drafts into poems. Your goal will be to teach children that poems are more concentrated than stories and that when poets have story-like drafts they make them more poem-like by eliminating unnecessary words and sections, choosing precise words, and adding colorful language.

THE MINILESSON

Connection

Remind the children of a time talking about kinds of something (kinds of dogs, horses, cars, music). Tell writers that you found they had written lots of kinds of poems.

"Yesterday during indoor recess, a few of you were looking at books about dogs and talking about all the kinds of dogs there are. You said there are," Stephanie began listing across her fingers, "dalmatians and golden retrievers and collies and poodles and great danes and cocker spaniels and flat-coated retrievers. Well last night, when I took your revision folders home and read all the poems in them, I realized there are lots of kinds of poems, too."

"I found some 'looking closely poems,' like 'Dogs,' by Hana." [*Fig. XIV-1*]

"And some 'funny poems,' like this one, by Anna." [*Fig. XIV-2*]

The connection in your minilessons will not always summarize the previous day's work in the writing workshop, sometimes instead, the minilesson will begin by calling to mind another conversation that will provide the foundation for today's new learning.

Dogs
Dogs sleeping
in a dog house.
little paws
moving
Back and forth.
The dog wakes up.
scatters to the kitchen
I feed it.
It thanks me.
A big lick
on my face.

Fig. XIV-1   Hana

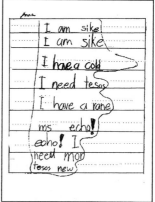

I am sick.
I am sick.
I have
a cold.
I need tissues.
I have a runny
nose. Achoo!
Achoo! I
need more
tissues now.

Fig. XIV-2   Anna

"And I found some 'story poems,' like this one, by Aidan."

When I learned how to ride my bike it
Was hard. I tried for a long time. I tried
And tried a lot.

I am going by myself. I can ride with
Other people now.

I am doing it! I can go with my friends
And bike along.

I am going faster than my dad!
I am going faster than my sister.

I can ride by myself.
I can do it! Yay.

"Today, what I want to suggest is that different kinds of poems need different kinds of revision. And I especially want to talk about one kind of poem. It seemed to me when I looked over your poems that most of you have some drafts of poems that could go in a category of not-yet-poems."

"*Many* (but not all) of your not-yet-poems could also be called stories. Today, I want to show you how you can take stories that aren't yet poems and revise them into story poems."

Perhaps because minilessons rely on spoken language and on learners taking information in through their ears, teachers sometimes borrow the cadences of orators, of speakers. You'll notice a lot of use of parallel structure, as in "different kinds of poems need different kinds of revision."

I love this section of a minilesson. How nice it is to have a teacher come right out and say in as explicit a fashion as possible what she hopes to teach. Always, the teaching point of a lesson needs to be one that writers can take with them to other days, other texts.

Teach

Tell the children about one child who found he had a story that wasn't yet a poem. He decided it was like weak lemonade and that, to turn it into the strong lemon juice of a poem, he rewrote it. Show the before and after versions.

"Daniel and I were looking through his revision folder yesterday, and he found he had one of those stories that wasn't yet a poem. It went like this:"

I went to the circus with my family.
We took the subway.

We waited in a line.
I got a bag of popcorn.
Everyone was clapping.
We saw guys flipping in the air.
We saw horses galloping over poles.
My dad told me we had to leave early.
I was tired and happy.

"It looked like a poem with line breaks and all, but Daniel told me it didn't feel strong enough to be a real poem." We decided that stories that aren't yet poems are like weak, watered-down lemonade. Have you ever tasted that? So Daniel decided to revise his draft to make it more like the really strong juice of a lemon. Have you ever sucked a lemon slice?" Stephanie reenacted how she would react to just a tiny taste of tart lemon!

"Look at Daniel's next draft. He's hoping he revised his story that wasn't yet a poem into a 'story poem.'"

OLD VERSION	NEW VERSION
I went to the circus with my family.	Munching popcorn from
We took the subway.	A bag
	Crowd applausing
We waited in a line.	Very loud
I got a bag of popcorn.	Guys flipping into
Everyone was clapping.	The air
We saw guys flipping in the air.	Like butterflies
We saw horses galloping over poles.	Horses clip
My dad told me we had to leave early.	Clop
I was tired and happy.	Jump over poles
	Gallop over obstacles
	I love the circus

It's fairly common for your minilesson to be built around a conference you had with one writer. As you confer, in the back of your mind you are often thinking, "Could other kids benefit from this same conversation?" If the answer is yes, you have two options. You might convene a small group for a strategy lesson (in this instance beginning, "Daniel and I just did some work together that I think might apply to all of you too"). Your other option is to bring the conference into the teaching component of a minilesson.

When we retell what happened in a one-to-one conference in a minilesson or a strategy lesson, we tend to tweak the real story just a bit to give the child credit for originating ideas that may actually have been ours. Instead of saying, "I told Daniel to . . ." we're apt to say, "Daniel got the idea to . . ." or "Daniel decided to. . . ."

Active Engagement

Ask the children to talk in their partnerships, naming particular things the child did to rewrite his story into a poem.

"So, writers, would you and your partner find three things Daniel did to change his weak lemonade into strong lemon juice, his not-yet-poem into a poem?" The room erupted with talk.

Recruit the class to make a chart listing steps writers take to turn stories into poems. Use the chart as a focus around which to elicit observations about what the one child has done.

Soon Stephanie reconvened the class. "So let's use Daniel's example to help us make a new chart." Stephanie wrote the heading "Turning Stories into Poems" on chart paper.

"What's one thing I could put on this chart? What might writers do to turn stories into poems?"

"Take out words?"

"You are on to something, Hana, but can you be more specific? Which words?"

"The extra ones."

"Do you all agree with Hana? Tell your partner some of the extra words Daniel took out of his poem."

"I heard some of you say that Daniel took out whole parts of his story that weren't the main thing. Should that go on our list?" The children nodded. "Okay. What else goes up here?"

The room was silent for a bit. Then Maddie's hand shot up. "Take out periods," she said.

When children suggest items that aren't yet exportable to other texts, help them rephrase their wording.

"Daniel did do that, but, Maddie, I don't think we can say poets always take out periods. Should we say it like this, 'Decide if you want sentences with periods or not?'"

Maddie nodded and this, too, went on the chart.

"What else?"

"Add parts?"

Assigning partners to "find three things Daniel did" sets them up to talk in an expository, list-like way. It's wise to help children channel their talk into either narrative or expository (list-like) structures. This is a good opportunity for them to practice talking in an expository (or list-like) way.

Moves like this, in which Stephanie recruits all children to respond to what one child has said, involve all the children in the conversation.

There are a few teaching methods we use repeatedly in the teaching and active involvement components of our minilessons. One of them is illustrated here. "Would you think about what you've just seen," we ask children, "and list things the writer did that all of us could do?" We're asking children to notice and to extrapolate the transferable thing a writer has done. In this instance, Maddie points to a specific thing the poet—Daniel—has done that is transferable only when it's described a bit differently. For this reason, Stephanie helps her to reword her observation of what Daniel did so that it can become part of a chart of recommended strategies poets can use.

Stephanie signaled for Klara to go on. She pointed to the section in which Daniel added that acrobats flipped like butterflies.

"Okay, all of you. We have a chart here that says—read it with me:

TURNING STORIES INTO POEMS
....

- Take out extra words (finally, then . . .)
- Take out parts of the story that aren't the main thing
- Decide if you want sentences with periods or not

"Now we're thinking what to put next. Klara helped us see that to turn his story into a poem, Daniel not only took out words, he also added the parts about acrobats flipping like butterflies and the horses clip-clopping. Should I put on the list that all of us can turn our stories into poems if we 'add that the guys flipped like butterflies,' and 'add that the horses clip-clopped?' Alex, what do you think?"

"Put 'add better words.'"

"Smart! You are right that poets don't always say 'guys flipped like butterflies' but they do write with better words. How can I describe those better words more exactly?"

"Add words that show, not tell?"

TURNING STORIES INTO POEMS
....

- Take out extra words (finally, then . . .)
- Take out parts of the story that aren't the main thing
- Decide if you want sentences with periods or not
- Add words to show, not tell

Link
Send the children off, showing them that today's lesson could guide them to revise or to write new poems that are more like lemon juice than lemonade.

"Today, some of you may want to sort through the poems you want to revise. If you find some get sorted into the pile of stories that aren't yet poems, you can use our chart to help you revise, turning these into poems. Remember, your goal is to make lemon juice . . . not weak lemonade."

Earlier, when Maddie's observation about deleting periods needed to be tweaked before it could go on the list, Stephanie did this work for her:"Should we say it like this?" This time, she involves the whole class in trying to restate Klara's suggestion. She scaffolds the process for them.

Alex's comment 'add better words' is half right while still not being specific. Stephanie supports the wise part of what Alex has done, then extends it. Notice, in fact, that Stephanie has coached each child to revise his or her suggestion so that it is more specific and precise.

In general, we have a saying, "Charting is not teaching." It's a mistake to get into the rhythm of making new charts every day and of recording every word that every child says. This minilesson, with its emphasis on "let's build a chart," is the exception, not the rule! The minilesson is worth studying, however, because Stephanie has made a number of teaching moves that are worth replicating. Just as the children have charted what Daniel did that is worth exporting, you could chart what Stephanie has done that is worth exporting to other minilessons. Start with:

- *Ask children to generate ideas for the chart in partner conversations*
- *When one child makes a suggestion, engage all children in talking back to that suggestion in one-to-one partner conversation. Preface this "Can you find an example of . . . talk to your partner."*

TIME TO CONFER

This minilesson has set you up for lots of wonderful conferences. My conference with Owen could suggest one possibility to you, and you also confer about anything you've taught in this unit or this year. Specifically, today's minilesson could lead you to:

▶ Notice what a child is doing to rewrite story-like drafts of poems, turning these into more poetic poems. You might suggest the child use the chart as a guide, checking off which thing she has already done and which she still plans to do. One of the larger lessons that you could extrapolate from this is that whenever a child is looking for guidance, one option is to use charts as teachers.

▶ Suggest a child could go back to publications from earlier in the year that were intended to be stories. Now, in the light of all the child now knows, could any of these be rewritten as poems?

▶ Notice what children are doing to turn not-yet-poems into poems and suggest that these children's actions mean new bullets need to be added to the chart.

▶ Point out that many children also have a pile of poems which they've identified as "Observation Poems" and teach them ways to revise those poems. These poems rely on poets seeing with fresh eyes (and avoiding clichés), on poets including sensory detail, and on poets having a message to say that provides them with a focus on a lens. If the message is that raindrops are like pearls, then only certain observations belong.

These conferences in *The Conferring Handbook* may be especially helpful today:

▶ *"Can You Think of One Moment That Holds the Big Feeling the Ocean Gives You?"*

▶ *"Are Those the Sounds You Hear?"*

▶ *"Can You Help Me See What You Saw?"*

Also, if you have *Conferring with Primary Writers*, you may want to refer to the conferences in part seven.

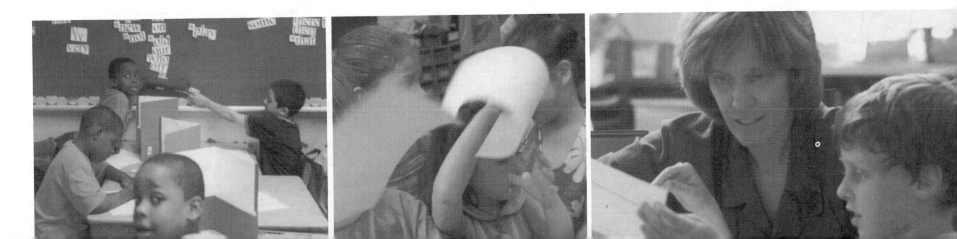

AFTER-THE-WORKSHOP SHARE

Tell the children that to prepare for the celebration they will need to choose pieces to publish and to plan the celebration. Have them set to work on the first of these.

"Writers, we need to send invitations home soon inviting your caregivers to our poetry celebration, but before we can do that, we need to plan how the celebration will go. So I was thinking that we need to do two things right now. First, you each need to select a small collection of poems that are your very best. We'll try to publish all of these. Then, we need to plan our celebration. So let's first take five minutes of quiet time.

"Would you each select a couple of poems you especially want to publish? I'll give you a purple paper clip, let's use it to clip together the poems we want to publish." The class got to work.

Enlist small groups of students to think of great ways to celebrate poetry.

"Writers, the next thing we need to do is to decide on *how* we could publish our poems. Usually I make this decision, but this time, I want to hear your ideas. So will two partnerships combine, making small groups of four poets, and will you think, 'What would make a great way to publish and celebrate our poems?'"

After five minutes of conversation, Stephanie reconvened the class and they began to share ideas. The class soon agreed their best idea was to inquire whether they could post their poems in the New York City subway cars. Through a program called Poetry in Motion, most of New York City's subway cars already display poems by published poets, and Stephanie's children wanted their poems displayed in a similar fashion. The children agreed, however, that if that wasn't possible, their next-best plan would be to post their poems on kiosks, subway tollbooths, city library bulletin boards, and store windows.

With this goal in mind, children went home with a letter asking their caregivers to help by volunteering time in the publishing center or by agreeing to participate in a "poem walk" through the neighborhood as part of their celebration.

Stephanie uses the word caregivers *in this instance. You'll need to decide what words you use to talk about the people children invite to their celebrations. Keep in mind that far too many children are asked to make Father's Day gifts for fathers they don't have. . . .*

Never underestimate the power of materials—even a single purple paper clip.

As the year progresses, the methods of publication need to change because each method has its own payoffs and lessons. Above all, you want to publish in ways that give children readers, and that help them feel as if they are writers.

IF CHILDREN NEED MORE TIME

Consider turning today's minilesson into a whole bend in the road. Almost everything you've taught thus far in the unit could be revisited under the umbrella of turning drafts that aren't yet poems into poems. Most important, you could:

- Extend the list you and the class created today by suggesting children recall earlier work in which you suggested poets see the world with fresh eyes and write/reread/write/revise to make the sounds of poems match their meaning.

- Show and discuss the results of one child who revised his or her draft of a poem to make it less story-like and more poetic.

- Suggest that children have drafts of other not-yet-poems in their folders. Some of these will be observations en route to becoming poems, and you could suggest that writers do similar (and different) work to turn observations into poems.

- Help children apprentice themselves to published poets, perhaps noticing especially the word choices those poets have made. Let these poets inform your children as they make final revisions on their own poems.

REVISING AND EDITING POETRY

GETTING READY

▶ Editing chart you have been building throughout the year (if you haven't been doing this, use copies of an editing checklist that reflects what you can expect from most of your children)

▶ Lines of poetry with some misspelled words—(it is best to get these from children's writing, but only with their permission

● See CD-ROM for resources

YOUR CHILDREN WILL EACH HAVE A HANDFUL *of poems they're determined to publish and plans to post those poems on subways, kiosks, library bulletin boards, and store windows. They'll enter the workshop with a renewed energy to work. Tap into this! Remind them that now they'll want to reread each poem asking, "Is this my best?"*

Your students already have a large repertoire of strategies for improving their writing. You'll remind them to use all these strategies, and you'll teach them to reread their poems, checking every single word to be sure it's spelled as correctly as it can be.

Because of its condensed nature, poetry is a perfect genre to teach children the importance of closely scrutinizing their writing to make sure each word is spelled accurately. Today you'll teach children to reread with pen in hand, carefully checking each word and then doing everything possible to fix words that require more attention.

THE MINILESSON

Connection

Give an example of a time when you had to make something look its best in a short amount of time.

"We had visitors at my house yesterday. My husband called to tell me he was bringing home lots and lots of people, and they were people I didn't even know. He said, 'They are coming in one hour.' I hung up the phone and looked around, and I bet you can guess what I thought. I thought, 'Uh oh! I better hurry. I've got to make this place look *really* good, *really* quickly.'"

"When we writers hear that our writing will be published soon, we hang up the telephone in the same way and we think, 'Uh oh! I better hurry! I've got to make this writing look really good, really quickly.'"

Tell the children that today you will teach them how to prepare their work for publication.

"So today, I want to teach you how we can clean up not our apartments but our poems."

Teach

Show the class some lines from student poems and tell them that the first step to cleaning up the work is to reread it slowly and carefully.

"When I want to clean up my poem (or my apartment), I go slowly through each part of it. I look at everything, slowly and carefully. I'll show you a few lines from Ramon's and Chloe's poems. Notice the kinds of things I 'clean up' when I am preparing a poem for company."

Never underestimate the power of metaphor. We've all experienced the rush to clean up quickly because company is coming. Why not help writers realize this is just what every writer does as we make last-minute repairs in preparation for readers. Often in this series, you see us describe the writing process and qualities of your writing by likening writing to something from our ordinary lives. For example, the beads in a necklace are patterned and poems, too, have patterns. Or, the example of often when you look through the trash, you find treasures… and poets, too, can look through discarded drafts and find words or phrases that are treasures.

"Here's what Ramon wrote:"

I saw three birds
A boy sprinkled bits of bread to the birds
The birds were talking.

"And Chloe wrote this:"

At the beach
Creepy crawlly insects going up your arm.

Demonstrate reading the work slowly, fixing errors as you go. Comment aloud as you correct spelling, particularly calling attention to spelling patterns and initial blends (or whatever new item you have decided to add to your editing checklist).

"Okay, first, I get out my pen. I read each word with my pen in hand. I'm specifically checking for blends and spelling patterns. I check the first word. *I*. Good, that's right. Now I check the next word. *saw*. That's right. Now *thee*. Hmm. I'm not sure. I want to say *three*. I need to add an *r*."

Reading on, Stephanie came to the word *sprinkled*, written as *spicold*.

"This word is supposed to say *sprinkled*, but it doesn't. Ramon has the *s* and the *p*, but I remember that that blend is tricky because it has three letters. There's an *r* there too, right? So I'm going to fix that."

"Now Chloe has a word with a spelling pattern we definitely know. This word is supposed to be *beach*, but it's missing the *a*. I'm going to fix this, too. Did you notice how I can look for blends and spelling patterns I know? *Sprinkled* might not be right yet, but I have made it better than it was before."

I show children's work that is reasonably correct because I want children to see me searching for things to fix up— and because I don't worry that these authors will feel undermined. If ever Ramon and Chloe have editing work to do, then all of us do.

Notice that as I reread, I didn't necessarily make every word perfect.

Add "blends and spelling patterns" (or your own new item) to your editing checklist.

"I'm going to add 'blends and spelling patterns I know are spelled right' to our editing checklist. Now it says:

- Reread
- Make sure all the words are there
- Words have spaces between
- There are no backwards letters
- Word-wall words are spelled right
- The punctuation is correct (periods, question marks, exclamation points, talking marks)
- Capitalization is correct
- Blends and spelling patterns are spelled correctly

Obviously, the list would be simpler if this were a class of kindergartners!

Active Engagement

Ask the class to look at the next few lines as carefully as you looked at the first ones, using the editing checklist as a guide.

"With your partner, use this checklist to help you edit the next lines from Chloe's and Ramon's poems."

Gaby: "*Bread* has an *r*, too. Ramon, do you have a little trouble with the blends that have an *r*?"

Ramon: "I guess a little."

Gaby: "I do too, so I always look extra hard for those ones when I'm editing."

Klara: "I know *birds* has an *i* in it from when I was writing nonfiction about birds."

Maddie: "And *talk* is *a-l-k*, just like *walk*."

Often in minilessons, the teacher demonstrates for a bit and then passes the baton to children and they continue where the teacher left off.

Link

Send the children off to edit their own poems, reminding them explicitly to use the new item on the list.

"As you go off to edit your own poems, remember to use whole editing chart, including this new thing."

TIME TO CONFER

Every unit you have taught includes sessions focused on editing. For today's conferences, you can turn back to any of these minilessons for tips on how to proceed. *Writing for Readers* especially has many minilessons that could help you conduct editing conferences.

As you confer with writers and hold strategy lessons, be on the lookout for prevailing editing issues that you could address in a quick, pointed bit of mid-workshop teaching. You might offer a quick reminder to consult the word wall to check spellings, or a reminder to use a partner to help find fixable parts you missed.

 These conferences in *The Conferring Handbook* may be especially helpful today:

▶ *"Can You Think of One Moment That Holds the Big Feeling the Ocean Gives You?"*

▶ *"Are Those the Sounds You Hear?"*

▶ *"Can You Help Me See What You Saw?"*

Also, if you have *Conferring with Primary Writers*, you may want to refer to the conferences in part seven.

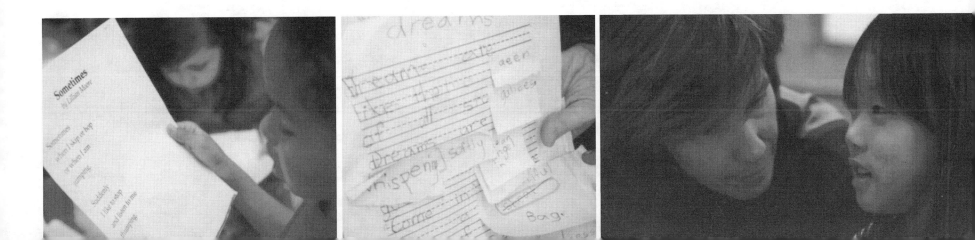

Help children practice reading their best poems aloud.

"Instead of sharing one or two poems today, I want to give us all a few minutes to practice reading our best poems out loud. We have talked a lot about the music of poetry and how better to give our poems that final amazing musical quality than to read them aloud with the love and care they deserve. Bring your poems to the rug and read them aloud to your partners. Read them as many times as you need to get that sound just how you like it."

PRESENTING POEMS TO THE WORLD: AN AUTHOR'S CELEBRATION

GETTING READY

▶ Permission for the children to take a neighborhood walk

▶ Plans for appropriate places to post particular poems

▶ Copies of poems and means to affix them

● See CD-ROM for resources

WHEN I WORK WITH ADULTS AND OLDER CHILDREN, *I often ask them to make timelines of themselves as writers: "Let's make timelines of our lives as writers. Put the moments that have mattered most into your timeline." Often, before we talk about our writing histories, I ask people to reflect on their timelines: "What have the turning points been in your writing life?"*

Time and again, people respond by telling about a time long, long ago, when their words were published. "I really felt like an author," they confide.

As teachers, we need to move heaven and earth to be sure every child knows what it is to be a published author. It's for this reason that you've gone to great lengths all year to celebrate your children's writing. Now, as this unit on poetry comes to an end, you'll want to design a finale that outdoes all the others. Invite your children to join in the fun. "What should we do?" you'll ask.

I've seen classrooms organize "coffee houses" that feature poetry readings. I've seen children use xylophones and recorders (and accompanying hand gestures) to set poems to music. I've seen classrooms decide to give poetry away, creating "literary gifts" that include framed poems and tape-recorded readings of poems. I've seen anthologies of all sorts and sizes.

In this celebration, you'll help children make their poems public by posting them in the community and reading them to various audiences.

THE CELEBRATION

Take the children to a place suggested by one of the poems. Have the student perform and post that poem while everyone listens.

Abuzz with excitement, the class headed to a kiosk in a nearby park, where Daniel posted his poem. The group gathered close, pulling in curious onlookers, and Daniel read his poem aloud.

"Trees"
Did you know that squirrels
Plant more trees than people?
They sometimes forget
Where they buried their food.
Digging.
Down in the ground
Deeper
And faster
He drops his food
Under the dirt.

A few days later
He forgets

A little sun
A little water
And BOOM!
A tree.

Stephanie's children had wanted to post their poems on the subways that crisscross our city, but this would have been something of a logistical nightmare. They were perfectly content (in fact, absolutely thrilled!) to revise their plans and instead publish their poems by distributing them to key sites around the neighborhood. The children and their families met at the school for a celebration breakfast and then headed into the world, poems in hand.

Continue with the trip, performing poems and leaving them behind as you all go. Afterward, post all the poems on a classroom bulletin board.

Then the group moved on to a nearby daycare center, where Madeline posted "When Isabel Was Born." Here, too, the posting was accompanied by a performance, by Madeline.

Waiting
For the baby
Mom took lots of walks
One day
The midwife came
Daddy tried to wake me
I was fast
Asleep

The baby came out
I finally woke up
She was crying
I got to hold her. She was
Soft, wet, slippery
With grease and blood
All over her
We looked in each other's eyes
She was smiling at me
Her name was Isabel.

The class delivered several more poems to appropriate spots—Eli's poem about eating lunch to the window of the neighborhood pizza store, Taylor's poem about feeling sick to the school nurse's bulletin board—and then went back to the classroom to post the rest of their poems on the class bulletin board for passers-by to read.